Battleground

REDAN RIDGE

Battleground Europe

REDAN RIDGE

Michael Renshaw

Great War series editor
Nigel Cave

Pen & Sword
MILITARY

First published in Great Britain in 2004 by
PEN & SWORD MILITARY
an imprint of
Pen & Sword Books Limited, 47 Church Street
Barnsley, South Yorkshire S70 2AS

ISBN 1 84415 055 0

Printed and bound in Great Britain by
CPI UK

Pen & Sword Books Ltd incorporates the imprints of
Pen & Sword Aviation, Pen & Sword Maritime, Pen & Sword Military,
Wharncliffe Local History, Pen & Sword Select,
Pen & Sword Military Classics and Leo Cooper.

For a complete list of Pen & Sword titles please contact:
PEN & SWORD BOOKS LIMITED
47 Church Street, Barnsley, South Yorkshire, S70 2AS, England.
E-mail: enquiries@pen-and-sword.co.uk
Website: www.pen-and-sword.co.uk

CONTENTS

Introduction by the Series Editor..6

Introduction...7

Chapter 1   **1 July 1916**...**11**

Chapter 2   **The November Battles – Monday 13 November** **45**

Chapter 3   **Wednesday 15 November**.....................................**61**

Chapter 4   **16-19 November**...**69**

Chapter 5   **Frankfurt Trench**..**81**

Chapter 6   **Visiting**...**101**

Chapter 7   **Somme Battlefields**..**109**

Chapter 8   **Walks and Tours**...**119**

          Index **173**

          Acknowledgements **176**

LIST OF MAPS

1. Relative British and German front lines. Page 13
2. Showing the objectives and timings for 4th Division 1 July.
   Note that Frankfurt Trench was to be captured after 45 minutes. Page 14
3. Assembly positions 4th Division 1 July. Page 16
4. Attack of 13 November. How the 2nd Division lined up. Page 46
5. The position mid-morning, 5 Brigade, 13 November. Page 53
6. The night of 13/14 November. Page 55
7. The attack of 14 November. Page 56
8. The 22/Royal Fusiliers clear the Quadrilateral. Page 62
9. 15 November. The 10/Loyal North Lancs position on the right. Page 64
10. 15 November. The position of the left of the attack. The 8/East Lancs
    between Lager Alley and Crater Lane. Page 65
11. 32nd Division's dispositions on 18 Novmber. Page 74
12. The attempted relief of the party cut off in Frankfurt Trench. Note the
    three dugouts marked on original map. (Walker Avenue was previously
    known as New Trench). Page 93
13. Superimposed French map with trench map on which the walks are based.
    Page 102
14. WALK 1 The German Front Line. Page 121
15. WALK 2 The British Front Line 1 July. Page 130
16. WALK 2 (Continued) The British front Line. Page 139
17. WALK 3 The November Battles. Page 155

Introduction by the Series Editor

With the publication of this book in the *Battleground Europe* series, the last part of the Somme front line on 1 July 1916 has been covered. The first of these books, on Beaumont Hamel, came out as long ago as 1994; it has taken a total of nine of them to cover the line and involved five different authors. We are looking forward in the future to produce further books in the series looking from the other side of the line; there are numerous excellent German regimental histories which give graphic accounts of the events in that tumultuous year for this sleepy corner of France.

The action at Redan Ridge was as dismal for the British army as practically anywhere else on that ghastly morning, 1 July. It tends to get overlooked because it lies between the two popular visiting areas of Serre and Beaumont Hamel. But it is a most evocative place, made poignant by the several, isolated and, with one exception, small cemeteries that can be seen from the top of the Ridge.

The events of 1 July were tragic; and for some time nothing much happened in this sector as the British ground their way forward further south to the German Second and then the German Third lines. The final throes of the Somme battle took place here in the poor weather and limited daylight of November. The action commencing 13 November was as much to satisfy Joffre as any particular British demand; and it certainly had its success. But the fate of the 16th Highland Light Infantry and its heroic stand was epic in quality, though hopeless of military success.

Redan Ridge is a featureless place, pleasant enough in the summer with its wide ranging views; but come the rains and cold of autumn it is a dismal spot, even today. What must it have been like after the pounding of the ground in November 1916? Today the occasional building can be seen in the distance, or one or other of the Crosses of Sacrifice that mark the CWGC cemeteries. Then there was nothing – a wasteland if ever there was one.

The Somme was an important battle; it did have long term consequences in the outcome of the war; but this battlefield must have seemed like a vision of hell to the men who fought here. They have had to wait for their story to be told in this series; and at last that delay has been rectified.

Nigel Cave
Collegio Rosmini
Stresa.

THE ROAD TO THE SOMME

The events of August 1914 at Mons when the British Expeditionary Force walked straight into the German forces and then into a headlong retreat was an unexpected shock to the nation. Until then there had been much talk and speculation about it being 'over by Christmas'. Field Marshal Lord Kitchener, though, saw it differently and had already embarked on a recruiting campaign to raise a new force of seventy divisions. The Mons disaster lent great emphasis to his campaign and a slow start was replaced by a surge of enthusiasm. Within three weeks the first hundred thousand were already in training and men flocked to the recruiting points, sometimes queuing all day to sign on, falsifying their age, not only by claiming to be older, but also many older men who had retired from the army turned up claiming a more youthful status!

Rupert Brooke seemed to speak for them all when he wrote *'Now God be thanked Who has matched us with His hour'*. By 1915 these new soldiers were feted wherever they went, cheered on by large groups of flag waving women and children. By the end of the year nearly 3,000,000 volunteers had been raised. There was, however, a chronic lack of officers and many were recruited straight from the Officer Training Corps at public schools and universities. Many were still only teenagers and 'qualified' only by dint of their class status together with their 'Cert A', a document that indicated that they had done some basic drill and some weapon training. Others were 'dug-outs', that is elderly officers brought out of retirement, while others were promoted NCOs who seemed to fit the role.

In December 1915 a conference was held at Chantilly, where initial proposals were made for a joint allied offensive both in the east and the west in 1916. Even at that stage, though, things were not well between the British and the French. For the British, further disappointment had occurred at Neuve Chapelle and Loos and there was a strong feeling that the British were not pulling their weight. Joffre, the French Chief-of-Staff, had also experienced defeat in the battles in Lorraine in 1914, but survived to lead his nation's armed forces, unlike Sir John French, who was replaced by Sir Douglas Haig. There was an immediate difference

Joseph Joffre

Sir Douglas Haig

of opinion between Joffre and Haig. Haig did not like the choice of Picardy for the offensive and considered that ground further to the north in Flanders strategically more suitable. Kitchener had always urged Haig to act independently of the French, although Joffre held command of the biggest army in the field.

Haig is probably the most notable of that much maligned group of men: First World War generals. He was fifty-four years old and had been an officer in the Boer war, he had also been at Khartoum, in South Africa and India. Born in Scotland, into the Haig whisky empire, he was educated at public school and Oxford University and was successful at Sandhurst and Staff College, if not particularly popular with his contemporaries. He had many qualities that made him eminently suitable for the job. He cut a handsome and impressive figure, immaculate and well presented. He was studious and sober, religious and patriotic. Most of all he was tough and calm under pressure, seemingly impervious to disaster and human suffering on a large scale. He was, though, only ever able to operate under the conditions and limitations that prevailed at the time.

Why, then, has he been so reviled as the architect of so much misery and suffering?

Well, there is the tendency for our race to look for scapegoats; in today's currency, to build the 'stars' up and then try and knock them down again. But there is more to it than that. Haig's greatest failing, possibly, was his inability to communicate. A dour and silent man, he was surrounded by those who were in awe of him and felt unable to tell him anything that they felt he may not wish to hear. Whether this was more imagined than real in those around him is hard to say. Certainly there were times when he showed real concern and involved himself directly in decisions affecting the front line troops as, for example, in his initial refusal to allow the November battles of the Ancre to go ahead because of the weather, until persuaded by his senior officers.

Although very different in background, Joffre had at least one similar characteristic to Haig. He, too, was very tough in the face of disaster and was able to remain cool under intense pressure. So the two men met and disagreed on the battle plan. To Haig it seemed that the Somme was not the appropriate place. There had been little action there and all the Germans had to do was to dig. This they did to great effect, with the assistance of prisoners of war from the eastern front,

8

establishing deep underground redoubts, barracks, munitions dumps and even hospitals. The defensive positions were always carefully constructed to maximum advantage and any weaknesses supported by additional considerations. Haig suggested an alternative in Flanders, backed by an amphibious landing on the coast. The claims that Haig lacked vision and was obsessed with cavalry are hardly born out here. Eventually, though, he had to agree to Joffre's plan, which initially was to open a massive front across sixty miles with thirty nine French divisions supported by twenty five British divisions. This war of attrition was intended to break the Germans' will to fight at exactly the place where they were the strongest. The psychology, at least, was sound.

Lieutenant General Erich von Falkenhayn, Chief of the German General Staff, also had plans for a major offensive. France had already suffered huge losses and he planned that this would continue and that France would be 'bled white' until it surrendered. Falkenhayn chose Verdun, a strong military base near the border with Germany and of symbolic significance to the French, just a hundred miles from Paris. The psychology was the same, but Falkenhayn got in first. On 21 February 1916 the French were caught by surprise, but Joffre was not immediately deflected from his task on the Somme. General Phillipe Pètain was appointed the defender of Verdun and division after division was sent into the battle. In February the British took over part of the French sector to allow their troops to go to Verdun, and the available French troops were then reduced to eighteen divisions.

The crisis at Verdun came during the latter part of May. There were repeated calls for the British to 'do something', but Haig in his meticulous way (to whom the responsibility for the Somme had now effectively passed) would not be rushed. A stormy meeting took place on 26 May when Joffre lost his temper. As a result plans for the attack were brought forward from August to July. The pressure on Haig was not yet relieved, though. On 1 June a further meeting was convened at Querrieu near Amiens, to which Joffre brought reinforcements. The French President, Poincairé and Prime Minister Briand turned up. Joffre also brought along General Foch, who was to be in charge of the now dwindling French contingent. Haig had to give way again, and agreed to

French President M. Poinciaré

9

Ferdinand Foch

attack on 25 June, leaving himself less than four weeks to be ready. By the middle of June pressure on Verdun was reducing, for while in the French army there were instances of mutiny, the German losses were also enormous and the will to carry on the stalemate and slaughter was on the wane.

Bad weather postponed the attack, as we know, until 1 July, but its affect on events at Verdun, if any, were marginal, except finally to reduce French contribution to eight divisions. In effect, the whole plan, to attack on a massive sixty mile front and sweep the Germans out of France with one blow was now reduced to a front of about thirty miles, to include the remains of the French sector astride the River Somme. A total rethink, at this stage, would seem to be the most probable outcome, but when taking into account the state of relations between the French and British, both had probably had enough of acrimonious meetings for the time being.

So what the wider plan was for the eventual Somme battle is hard to determine, except that it was necessary for the British to be seen to do something. But at what a cost that proved to be.

French Prime Minister Briand

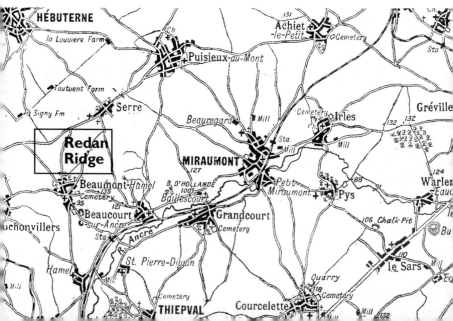

CHAPTER ONE

1 JULY 1916

There was some optimism on the eve of the battle. Surely, nothing could survive the massive bombardment that had been inflicted on the enemy positions. Some troops were told to walk over No Man's Land, carrying their rifles at the port position pointing into the sky and there seemed no reason to leave essential equipment behind, so many were loaded up with picks, shovels, barbed wire and other consolidating gear.

After all the rain, the day was fine and sunny, just right for a stroll after being cooped up in the trenches for days on end. Among the men of the 4th Division were some survivors from the original British Expeditionary Force, described by the German high command as that 'contemptible little army' whose losses had then been made up by Territorial troops. However, subsequent drafts of Kitcheners 'new army' recruits meant that for the most part the battalions involved bore no resemblance to their well trained predecessors.

The divisional formation was as follows:

10 Brigade:
1/R.Warwicks; 2/Seaforth H; 1/Royal Irish Fus. 2/R. Dublin Fus.

11 Brigade:
1/Somerset LI; 1/East Lancashire; 1/Hampshire; 1/Rifle Brigade.

12 Brigade:
1/King's Own; 2/Lancashire Fus; 2/Essex; 2/Duke of Wellington's.

Close by, on the right of the divisional sector on the other side of the

A British 9.2 gun on a railway mounting.

Beaumont-Auchonvillers road and on the left of the 29th Divisional sector, preparations had been made to blow a massive mine that had been laid under the German position known as the Hawthorn Ridge Redoubt and it is worth considering the effect of this plan and its consequences. The 252 Tunnelling Company of the Royal Engineers had dug a tunnel from a forward trench named Pilk Street and placed 40,000 pounds of ammonal in a chamber at the end of it. How to proceed with this feat of purely manual labour was, though, of some dispute. Lieutenant-General Sir A G Hunter-Weston, commanding VIII Corps, originally intended to blow it some hours before zero, occupy the crater, which would be in No Man's Land, and let the commotion die down before the main assault. In this way, it was hoped that the Germans would not be alerted to the imminent attack. Sir Douglas Haig, though, after consulting with the Inspector of Mines, overruled this, stating that the army's record at this tactic was poor while, by comparison the Germans were very adept at occupying craters and holding on to them. In all likelihood it would be the Germans who would be in possession of the position at zero hour. It had previously been ordered by Fourth Army Headquarters that all mines on its front should be exploded between zero and eight minutes before zero. Hunter-Weston, probably in a show of defiance, then suggested ten minutes before zero, though what difference two minutes would make is not clear, apart from 'face saving'. There was then some concern that the fallout from explosion would land on the attacking troops. However they would have had to have been lying out very close to the German lines for this to occur as it was already known from previous operations in Belgium that debris falls to the ground very quickly, at the maximum after about twenty to thirty seconds.

There was, then, the question of the artillery. This would have to lift in time to allow the assaulting troops to occupy the crater without hindrance. There was, though, to be more controversy. It was decided that all the heavy artillery in the entire 29th Division sector should lift from the front line at 7.20 am and shell the German reserve positions. There they would be joined by the howitzers, who were firing on the German second line, at 7.25 am. The small 18 pounder guns were ordered to reduce their fire by half at three minutes before zero. Thus, the Germans were forewarned and left largely unhindered to face their attackers. The diary of the VIII Corps Heavy Artillery states that the barrage lifted 'at 7.20 am and 7.25 am in accordance with operation orders' but many infantrymen claimed it lifted earlier than that. Later, though, no copy of the orders could be found.

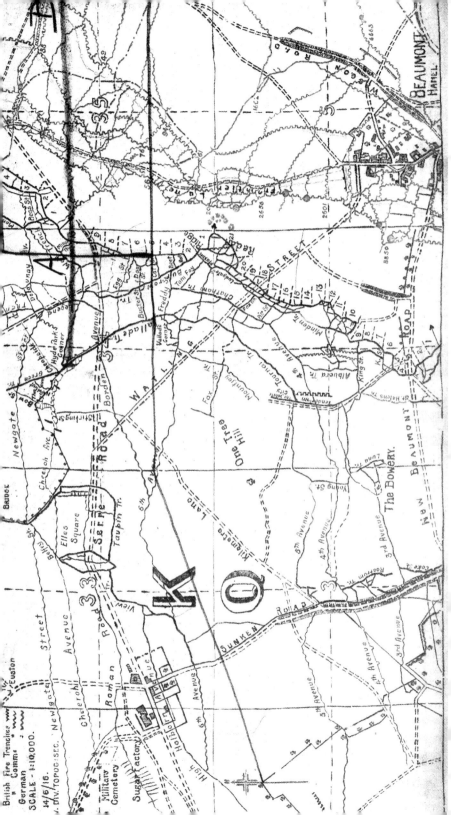

The men of the 4th Division, on the right of their sector on the Redan Ridge, could have had a 'grandstand' view of the events as they unfolded while they waited for their attack to commence. They would have seen two platoons of the 2/Royal Fusiliers rush forward with four Lewis guns and four Stokes mortars. They were greeted by heavy machinegun and rifle fire, and many were casualties before they reached the crater. Nevertheless, at least two Lewis gun positions were set up, one at each end of the crater, where they hung on. Eventually, they were driven back and later the Germans were seen out in No Man's Land making downward thrusts and it is thought that they were bayoneting the wounded.

A German account stated:

During the bombardment there was a terrific explosion which for a moment completely drowned the thunder of the artillery. A great cloud of smoke rose up from the trenches of no. 9 company, followed by a tremendous shower of stones, which seemed to fall from the sky all over our position. More than three sections of no. 9 company were blown into the air, and the neighbouring dugouts blown in and blocked. The ground all around was white with the debris of chalk as if it had been snowing, and a gigantic crater, over fifty yards in diametre, and sixty feet deep gaped like

Map 2. SHOWING THE OBJECTIVES AND TIMINGS FOR 4 DIVISION 1 JULY. NOTE THAT FRANKFURT TRENCH WAS TO BE CAPTURED AFTER 45 MINUTES.

(Taken from original colour coded map)

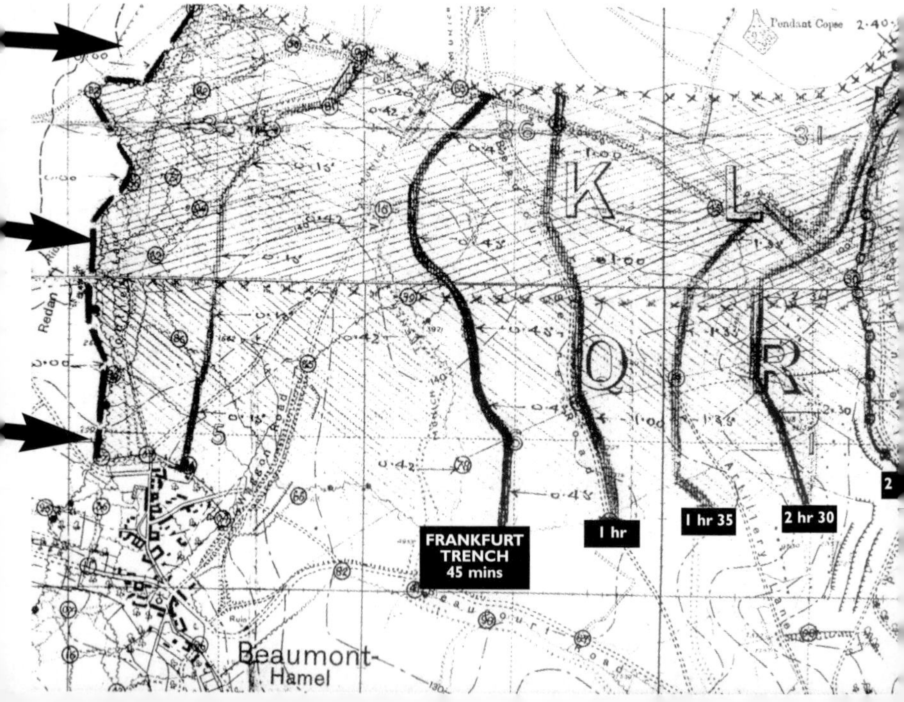

British troops await zero hour.

*an open wound in the side of the hill. The explosion was a signal
for the infantry attack, and every one got ready and stood on the
lower steps of the dugouts, rifles in hand, waiting for the
bombardment to lift. In a few minutes the shelling ceased, and we
rushed up the steps and out into the crater positions. Ahead of us
wave after wave of British troops were crawling out of their
trenches and coming forward towards us at a walk, their
bayonets glistening in the sun. (Reserve Regiment 119)*

Meanwhile, up on the Redan Ridge, because of the immense noise of
the barrage, the detonation of the mine went unheard, only those who
actually saw the explosion realising that it had occurred. As many of
the men were either crouching in their trenches or lying down close to
the ground out in No Man's Land, it went largely unnoticed by the men
of the 4th Division, as did some of the smaller mines blown in their
sector. The ground across which they had to attack was completely
open, without a scrap of cover, and from the right sloped up to the left
until it reached the top of the ridge, where the Germans had
constructed a large defensive position which dominated the area from
all directions. The British marked this as Ridge Redoubt on their maps.
The ground then sloped more gently to the left and there was some

'dead' ground, that is ground that could not be covered by fire from Ridge Redoubt near the divisional boundary with the 31st Division. However, this area was confronted by another strongpoint, a salient known as the *Quadrilateral* to the British troops and the *Heidenkopf* to the Germans, apparently named after one of their senior officers.

The story of the attack in broad terms can be recorded quite briefly. It failed because of intense machine gun fire which was already pouring on to the attacking troops before 'Zero'. On the right of the attack (to the south) below the redoubt no one got into the enemy front line, except one small party of 1/E Lancs who got into a communication trench leading to the German second line, but they were never heard of again.

On the left (to the north) of the attack, where the ground was slightly more favourable, the German front line and the Quadrilateral were occupied. The communication trenches between the front and second line were filled with men of various regiments and some of the second line was also taken. Further north, right on the divisional boundary, some men of the 8 and 6/Royal Warwicks (the latter loaned from the 48th Division), 1/Essex, 2/Lancs Fusiliers and 1/King's Own, broke through and, reinforced by some men of a Northern 'Pals' battalion, possibly the Leeds Pals, as they were the closest, advanced

Map 3. ASSEMBLY POSITIONS, 4 DIVISION 1 JULY. (Taken from original colour coded map)

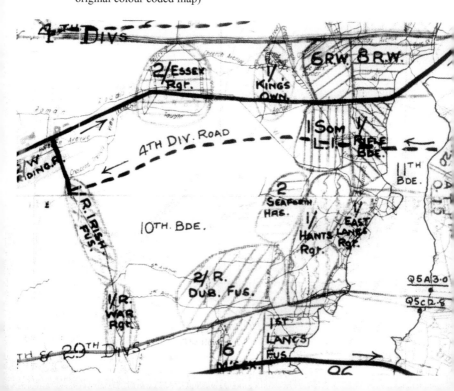

A German Maxim crew await the attack.

German troops take British prisoners.

to Pendant Copse, a small wood behind the village of Serre and well beyond the German second main position known as Munich Trench. They were never seen again. Air reconnaissance reported this as a breakthrough and as a result false hopes were raised.

The reason there were so many mixed units in the communication trenches north of Ridge Redoubt was because many men veered sharply to the left away from the more concentrated fire on the right, which also came from the Hawthorn Ridge in front of Beaumont Hamel. Ridge Redoubt itself bristled with machine guns but the enfilade fire from the Hawthorn Ridge just destroyed any units trying to cross that exposed ground to the left of the redoubt.

That then summarises the events of 1 July on Redan Ridge, but there is some interesting detail and individual endeavours to note, not least the award, subsequently, of a Victoria Cross. The dispositions of the 4th Division for the attack were made on a three battalion front.

Commencing from left to right on the 31st Divisional boundary;

Front Line: 8/Royal Warwicks; 1/Rifle Brigade; 1/East Lancs.

In Support: 6/Royal Warwicks; 1/Somerset L I; 1/Hampshire; 1/King's Own; 2/Lancs F; 2/Seaforth H; 2/Royal Dublin F.

In Reserve: 2/Essex; 2/Duke of Wellington;1/Royal Irish F; 1/Royal Warwicks. (See Map 3, page 16).

The initial objective was for the front line troops to secure Beaucourt Trench and for the first support battalions to 'leap-frog' them and capture Munich Trench beyond.

Starting with the attack on the right with the 1/East Lancs, this was made on a three company front. On the right C Company was led by Captain Thomas. A Company in the centre was commanded by Captain Penny. On the left Captain Browne was in charge of B Company. In reserve D Company

Sergeant Henry Hargreaves, 1/East Lancs, from Burnley, was killed in action 1 July 1916. He is commemorated on the Thiepval Memorial.

was led by Captain Hatfield.

As already explained, the artillery were to lift the barrage early to allow the Hawthorn Crater to be occupied; by the time the East Lancs were in position in No Man's Land, the German machine guns were already in action. Prior to the attack, patrols had gone out into No Man's Land on two occasions and found the wire uncut and that is how the attack faltered. Many men surviving the journey across were cut down trying to find a way through. Lance Corporal McDonald had been detailed to go across with A Company, taking a telephone and a reel of wire. Lieutenant Colonel Green, the Commanding Officer, went with his headquarters staff, following the wire which led them to a shell hole amid the German wire but short of the

Lieutenant Colonel J S Green DSO.

front line trench where Lance Corporal McDonald was lying. Green was shot through the shoulder but refused to be taken back and remained at his post. He had counted at least eight machine guns firing on the battalion front. After cutting more wire, battalion headquarters was established there. Just a few men of B Company actually passed into the German position on the left, near Ridge Redoubt, but they were insignificant and, these apart, no one got any further forward than a line of shell holes in front of the wire. Darkness allowed those able to do so to crawl back. On the way back, at 6.00 pm, the Adjutant, Captain Heath, was seriously wounded and was left behind but Lieutenant Colonel Green got in at 8.30 pm.

Captain Thomas had been killed leading the attack, Captain Browne had been taken prisoner and Captain Penny was missing. The Medical Officer, Captain Whigam, did excellent work along with his orderly Lance Corporal Brightmore, but was shot in the shoulder while tending the wounded in No Man's Land and was taken back.

The Battalion had gone into action that morning with twenty two officers and 680 other ranks and by that evening, ten officers had been killed. A further eight had been wounded, one was missing, leaving just three unscathed. Of the men, 160 had been killed, 238 were wounded and forty were unaccounted for, a total of 430.

Captain Browne was well treated by the Germans. He was lying wounded in a shell hole and was having grenades thrown in his direction, probably by men of the 1/Hampshires who were supporting the attack. This ceased, however and later he intended to crawl back, but in the evening a German private came out and hauled him in. As he was helped down into the German trench he looked back over No Man's Land and 'saw that a broad stretch of it was coloured khaki by the British dead and wounded which carpeted the ground'.

Earlier, Captain Browne had been hit in the thigh and his runner Private Laverack helped him dress the wound. Captain Penny arrived; he, too, had been wounded twice. He left in search of his own company. Browne, having got behind the advance, sent Laverack forward to see what was happening.

He had hardly left me, and I was still preparing to follow him, when he was back, saying, "They're being counter attacked, Sir, and what is left of them are coming back". Practically at the same moment we were joined by ten or a dozen men from the front who, however, at once stopped and opened fire on the Germans who now showed themselves in numbers. I went off to

German machine gun crew in action.

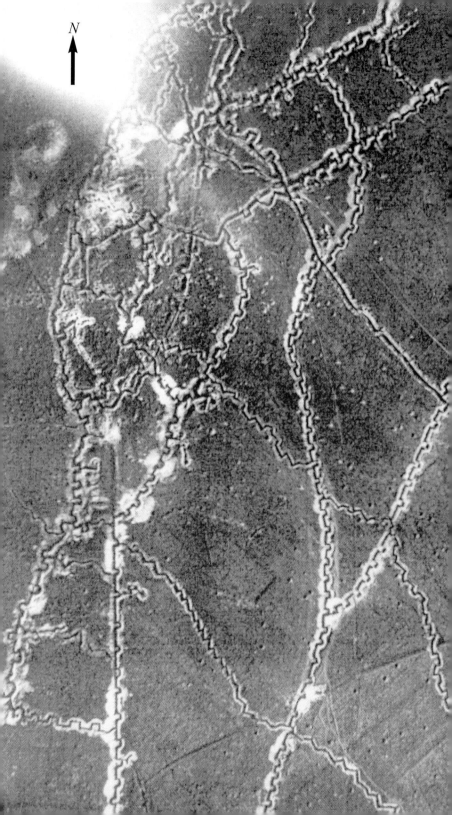

Redan Ridge No.2 Cemetery

Beaumont Church

View today af the embankment in Watling Street where Lieutenant Shearn lay wounded. Beaumont-Hamel is in the background.

the left to try and find more of our men but found no one, was wounded again by a ricochet and finally forced to take refuge alone in a shell hole.

Browne spoke good German and one man said to him: 'You English had to give the New Army you made a trial. You have done so and it has failed. Now we shall have peace!'

Another complained that his arm was very stiff from throwing grenades.

One of the three East Lancs officers unwounded was Second Lieutenant W J Page. He was the Battalion Intelligence Officer. He wrote that the battalion was met by intensive fire of artillery of various calibres and intensive enfiladed machine gun fire. D Company were being hit as they got out of the trench onto the parapet. He went out into No Man's Land followed by Lieutenant Newcombe, Battalion Machine Gun Officer:

I lacked his great coolness. I proceeded at a half run. "Newky" walked coolly along, took out his case and lighted a cigarette. A minute or so later he met a bullet and dropped dead in his paces.

Lieutenant R Newcombe

Page continued forward and in about eight minutes after zero reached the German wire, which was solid and uncut. He saw a small group of German infantry standing on their parapet waving their caps on the wooden handles of their grenades and shouting 'Come on English'. He shot at the group with his revolver, but almost immediately a British shell landed right on top of them. He decided to dig in and was joined by Second Lieutenant Daly, who said that the situation was hopeless. Any movement from the wounded in No Man's Land induced a hail of bullets, so it was decided to lie there quietly in the heat of the day and await nightfall. They lay, with their men, motionless all day within a few yards of the Germans who, had they realised the presence of these men, could have despatched them all with just a few grenades.

Darkness fell and Page organized the withdrawal of the men before he and Daly set out.

The fall of a day like 1 July can bring no night in our accepted sense, just darkness on the same awful scene, like dusk coming down on a leaf strewn lawn in autumn time. But most of the leaves on the Somme fields lay still; some turned, some murmured in pain. Such was the scene as the last two men in the Regiment turned from their objective – and incidentally their home since 6.30am – the German wire. They stepped between the leaves. Occasional voices spoke a dying word. Some were placed in shell holes in the hope of just a little cover for a short time. But the position of the two fugitives was difficult indeed; they were endeavouring to return to their taking off trenches, but could do nothing but meander from one groaning figure to another, and give a word of hope and cheer, trying to take a course for the British lines, encircled in a perfect ring of Very lights and explosions of every kind...Suddenly the sound of a well known voice was heard. Captain S J Heath, the Adjutant...He was terribly wounded in the arm and leg. From him some idea of position was gained. He had wandered north and was lying

View today of the site of the Quadrilateral taken from near the British front line occupied by the 1/Somerset L I and the 2/Seaforths.

Site of Quadriateral

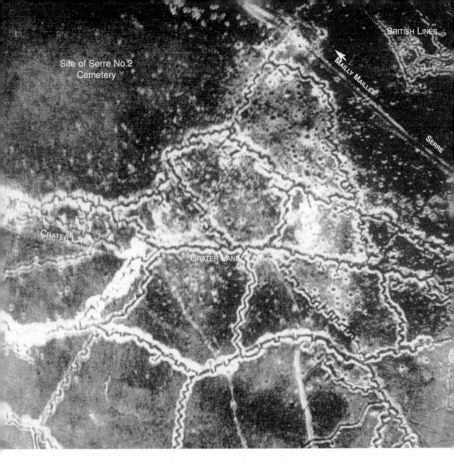

Aerial view of the Quadrilateral circa 1916.

opposite the Redan, which had been in the Rifle Brigade sector.
The two men finally made it back to the British lines and Second
Lieutenant Page went back to bring in Captain Heath with the
assistance of a volunteer private from the Royal Irish Fusiliers.
Lieutenant Daly collapsed on arrival.

Immediately following the East Lancs, at zero plus 10 minutes, the
1/Hampshires just telescoped into the rear of the north countrymen.
There was nothing to do except take refuge in the mass of shell holes
created by the massive German barrage and the two battalions became
hopelessly mixed up.

Not much is recorded about the 1/Hampshires but Lieutenant E D
Shearn was one of their officers who went over leading the assault and
he has left us with the following account;

As soon as I got out of the assembly trench I discovered that
the story that there would be nothing left alive in the German
lines was a myth. We went into literally a hail of machine gun

24

fire. I could hear the "smack" of the bullets as they hit the ground or sandbags or whatever. I got hit on my prismatic compass which I carried on the left front of my belt. I felt the impact of the bullet, I did not however feel pain or unwell. I thought it as well to look and see what damage had been done so I opened my belt and pulled up my shirt to see. There was a small and very neat hole under my left ribs from which a little blood was coming. I debated briefly whether I needed medical attention but decided that as I felt so unaffected by the bullet wound I had better get on with the war. I make no claim that I am in any way brave but I do distinctly remember feeling some surprise and indeed some satisfaction that I did not feel afraid. I did my belt up and hurried to catch up with my platoon. I saw Donald Day, a friend of mine, on my left. I noted with a slight feeling of amusement that he had his head down as though it were raining. It certainly was, so far as machine gun fire was concerned. I also remember greeting my company commander, Tommy Fawkes, with a salute. He said, "Don't be a bloody fool, you'll get me shot".

Shortly after this I crossed a sunken road at a tangent, down one side and up the other (Watling Street). *The road ran diagonally across our line of advance. Donald Day had by this time been hit in the knee and he was being helped to the comparative shelter of the further bank of the road by three other ranks. I chased two of them off him and got them to advance with me towards the German front line. I suppose I should have collected all three, but I left one to help Donald. I had got ten or fifteen yards past the sunken road when "smack", I felt as though something had hit me in the back I spun round in a half circle and came down on my bottom with my legs in the air and a feeling like pins and needles running down my right leg. I said aloud "That's it!". I think I intended to convey that I thought I was done for. It slowly dawned on me that it was very silly to keep my legs in the air where they might get in the way of a machine gun bullet, so I lowered them. My next thought was of Donald Day in the relative safety of the sunken road. I crawled there on my hands and knees and found that I had aimed correctly as I got down into the road pretty well*

Lieutenant Colonel The Hon. Lawrence Palk DSO, commanded 1/ Hampshires, killed in action 1 July, leading his men into action carrying nothing but a walking stick.

25

alongside of him. Some other rank got my field dressing and plugged my back, after pouring iodine into my wound. After he had done this he discovered bullet wounds in my right bicep which he treated with more iodine. When he had done so I enquired with a degree of misplaced humour "Is that the lot?".
"The lot" he exclaimed, "You've got a 'ole in your back you could put 'alf your 'and in!".

In the centre of the divisional front were the 1/Rifle Brigade. Two tunnels, Cat and Rat had been dug, reaching to within ten yards of the German front line. At zero the men advanced and on the right of the attack, especially, encountered very heavy machine gun fire from Ridge Redoubt. Two gun crews actually had their guns on the parapet of their trench, quite exposed, and continued to fire, sweeping the opposing trenches and lines of advancing troops until forced to take refuge by the advancing troops who somehow survived them. Another two, firing directly from the redoubt, continued to do so all day and were never silenced. Here, no penetration of the German front line was made, the men taking cover in the shell holes but, further to the right, in the vicinity of the tunnels, the men were out of the exits and through some gaps in the wire and into the German front line. Eventually the Germans, realising what was happening, organized a counterattack,

The Warwicks assemble prior to the attack.

coming out of their trench and attacking the exits. Lieutenant Robson gathered some men together and quickly engaged them and a close quarter fight ensued. It was, however, an unequal contest and the men of the Rifle Brigade were driven off. The Germans then blew up the exits to the tunnels.

The company in the centre of the attack were able to get into the German line and were favoured by having to pass to the left of Ridge Redoubt and the complex of old mine craters that lay in No Man's Land in front of it. There was little fire from the right from the Quadrilateral and they went through the gap, fighting through a complex of communication trenches and keeping direction quite well, veering only slightly to the left, eventually established themselves at the first objective looking across to Munich Trench. They had been followed into the attack by the 1/Somerset Light Infantry, who lost their commanding officer, Lieutenant Colonel Thicknesse, and their adjutant before the British front line was reached. Some units reached the first objective, also passing between Ridge Redoubt and the Quadrilateral towards Beaumont Trench, while further units of that battalion extended that position northwards.

Lieutenant Colonel Donald Wood, commanded the 1 Rifle Brigade. Killed 1 July, his body was never identified and he is commemorated on the Thiepval Memorial.

Sergeant A H Cook was among the first Somersets over the top and left us with this account of his fortunes:

The first line had almost reached the German front line, when all at once the machine guns opened up all along our front; fired with a murderous fire, and we were caught in the open, with no shelter; fire was directed on us from both flanks, men were falling like ninepins, my platoon officer fell (2nd Lt Tilley) he was wounded and captured. My platoon sergeant was killed which left me in charge of the platoon, this within five minutes of our advance.

We had to swing slightly to our left as to approach our objective direct was impossible, it meant going over some high ground which was being enfiladed by M.G. fire. I led the platoon on to the German first line, and after a breather went on to the second line. Here I lost control, the men were rushing here and there, from one shell hole to another, in their advance. The ground was covered with our dead, enfilade fire from the right played havoc with us all. Our guns had made an unholy mess of the German trenches, but very few dead could be seen, owing to the fact they were safely stowed away in their dugouts. Scarcely a square foot of ground had been left undisturbed, everything was churned up, there were huge gaps in the wire entanglements, but the dugouts were all practically safe. These were a revelation to us being most elaborately made, and down about thirty feet.

Mopping up parties were not clearing the trenches properly, as Jerry was popping up all over the place, behind and on our flanks and throwing grenades at us from all angles. A lot were seen to throw their hand in and were scattering back to our lines, but the majority were mown down by their own guns. It was impossible to get any further without help. Rumour said that some had reached their objectives and were now cut off. Dead and dying were lying everywhere, there was one man just in front of us sitting on a mound shouting for help, he was covered with blood from head to foot. There was a peculiar position here, the ground in front was circular in shape, or nearly so, it must have been the "Quadrilateral," as it was defended on all sides and about the size of Piccadilly Circus. Communication trenches were everywhere, and just in front was a communication trench up which some British troops were moving. This seemed quite in order until I noticed some Germans with fixed bayonet, and then I realised that our fellows were prisoners, so I started picking off the escorts; this was very successful, and quite good fun being able to hit back, although I seemed to be the only one chancing my head over the top. Our men could have escaped, but I suppose they were fed up with it all, and only too glad to be out of the fighting. The troops were very discouraged at being held up. The 10th and 12th Brigades reinforced us, but they were met by withering fire and practically annihilated. Their wounded were everywhere, and the dead were heaped on top of each other, where the machine guns had caught them.

Other units of both regiments found themselves opposite the south face of the Quadrilateral, but before they could make a decisive move there was a large explosion. The dust, debris and fallout from this made visibility very poor on the whole of the left hand side of the divisional sector and men of all regiments stumbled forward into the descending gloom.

The Germans had decided not to attempt to defend the salient but had constructed a mine which was intended to explode when the

British attacked. There was a single machine gun to lure the attackers forward but this jammed and was inoperable. Possibly in their haste to depart the sappers blew the mine early and so the Quadrilateral fell almost without a shot being fired. The whole area was wrecked. All the tunnels and dugouts were blown in and of no purposeful use to the British. However men poured into the position which acted like a magnet throughout the day. The Germans in the area between their front line and Beaumont Trench were overcome and it was at the latter position they made their stand before retreating to Munich Trench where they prepared for a counter attack.

Lieutenant Glover of the 1/Rifle Brigade was among those troops who passed north of Ridge Redoubt and veered to the left. At first, things seemed to be going quite well, but bunching began to occur, and as the German line was reached things changed:

The most fearsome hail of rifle and machine gunfire with continuous shelling opened up on us. Most of us seemed to be knocked out. There were some Germans in the trench nearby and Sgt Smith, Corprl. Halls and myself started to bomb, but the Germans cleared out to our right. What was left of us now seemed to get into the trench and a few Somersets came along and joined, a few going on farther but getting into shell holes just beyond. As far as I could judge we were in the German second trench in about A Coy's area.

Major G W Barclay MC, 1/Rifle Brigade, survived on I July but was killed in action four weeks later. Lieutenant Glover, after he was wounded and evacuated to England, wrote a long letter to Major Barclay describing the account of the fighting in the Quadrilateral. Whether he read it before he was killed is doubtful as it was attached to the Battalion diary.

Glover was indeed in Beaumont Trench and, as already mentioned, was reinforced by some Somersets who, unable to get any further towards Munich Trench than their shell holes, consolidated and extended their position northwards in an attempt to link up with the Warwickshire battalions which had attacked on the left.

I now found I was with CSM Selway and Sgt Hunt and together with them and Sgt Smith tried to strengthen our position, as we had no touch on the right and there was no possibility of going on. We were enfiladed too from the left but some Warwicks came up and apart from shelling we were fairly comfortable, Trevor turned up and Greetham of the Somersets and we decided to carry on, stretch out our right as far as we

Major Townsend, 8th Warwicks was mistakenly arrested a spy by Lieutenant Sherwood of the 7th Warwicks 2 May 191 Townsend liked his drink and was liable lead astray any junio officer who fell into path and it was felt t he set a bad example He was made salvag officer for 48th Division.

could, with Bn. Bombers, about half a dozen, on our right flank.
We will leave Lieutenant Glover for the time being, and look at the detail of the last of the battalions that were first across No Man's Land, the 8/Royal Warwicks and their sister battalion, the 6/Royal Warwicks. At first, as ordered, they walked forward, but Captain Martin, commanding A Company, ran through from the fourth line to the front

The Seaforth Highlanders man a Lewis gun post.

wave and got the men to run. Quite a number of the men from Birmingham were territorials and well trained. The left companies of 8/Royal Warwicks were hampered by fire from the village of Serre and the north end of Munich Trench. Captain Martin organized a party of men under the command of a young officer to move down a communication trench to the left, towards Serre, with the intention of attacking the machine guns firing from that direction. The party got cut off and were surrounded and Martin, under heavy attack from his right, could do nothing to assist, although he could see the frantic signals of a yellow flag. On the right, though, better progress was made and an entry was made into the German front line. Here hand to hand fighting took place, and the German troops had to give ground and the first objective, Beaumont Trench was reached, although there was no contact on the right. All this had been supported by the second Warwickshire battalion who left their positions at zero plus 10 minutes. The cost in casualties had been very high, though, and not enough support was forthcoming to enable a further advance to be made at that point. Contact was made eventually with the Rifle Brigade and the Somersets on the right. The Warwickshire men found themselves opposite a German strongpoint known as *Feste Soden,* near Munich Trench. Later the men, joined by others of various battalions, collected all the grenades they could find, both British and German, and crossed the redoubt and advanced on Frankfurt Trench.

The 8/Royal Warwicks Commanding Officer, Lieutenant Colonel Innes, was killed almost immediately, between the second and third British lines and also among very heavy officer casualties was the Adjutant, Lieutenant Procter. At the end of the day only one officer remained unscathed, Second Lieutenant Laing. Three of the Company Commanders were dead, Major Caddick commanding D Company had the misfortune to step on a booby trap and the fourth, Captain Martin, carried on while wounded. An unnamed officer with Captain Martin carried a Winchester repeater rifle into battle. The second in command of the Battalion, Major Townsend, was Australian by birth, but had settled in Birmingham, in business. He carried a Browning automatic into the battle with him, a bottle of whisky and a terrier dog. He lost direction but got into a German trench where he carried on the fight. He was wounded twice and returned to the British lines for more whisky. He was, however, bundled protesting into an ambulance. Such lighter moments, though, were rare. Of the other ranks 573 out of about the 600 that went over were casualties. That is over 95%. The 10/West Yorks, a Leeds battalion, suffered the greatest number of casualties on

1 July but in percentage terms a greater figure has not been found. The story was little better with the 6/Royal Warwicks with similarly only one officer unwounded, Second Lieutenant Cooper, who managed to get back with a message.

Because of the confusion and very heavy casualties it was decided to postpone the advance of further supporting battalions until the situation became clearer. The second wave of support battalions was due to go over at 9.30 am. The message delaying this was sent at 8.35 am from divisional headquarters but did not arrive in time to prevent them from doing so, as they had already begun to move forward towards the British front line from their positions in the rear. On the left the 2/Duke of Wellington's and the 2/Essex, who had been in reserve, were on their way and were moving so quickly that the runners carrying the messages were unable to prevent the 2/Essex from attacking. The Dukes leading right company, led by Captain Millin, also went over, the remaining companies being halted. The other battalions further forward, later reported that they never received the message at all. So even before 9.30 am, in some instances, a further four battalions plus half a battalion of 2/Lancashire Fusiliers and one company of Dukes rushed forward into the remains of six decimated battalions on a 1,200 yard frontage. At 9.00 am, on the right, the leading waves of the 2/Royal Dublins ran straight into heavy machine gun fire and the commanding officer, seeing that his leading men were held up in the congestion in No Man's Land among the East Lancs and the Hampshires, stopped any further attacks. Some of the Dublins got as far as Watling Street, the track that ran diagonally across No Man's Land.

Major J N Bromilow commanded the King's Own (Royal Lancaster Regiment). He was listed as missing; however, his body was later found and identified in August 1917. He is buried in Serre Road Cemetery No.1.

Lieutenant VFS Hawkins, 2/Lancashire Fusiliers, at 12 Infantry Brigade HQ reported:

Meanwhile we were waiting at Brigade Headquarters for news. The Essex and King's Own were going over first with the Lancashire Fusiliers, the Dukes in support. The King's Own and the Essex were wonderful. The King's Own got very nearly to Pendant Copse and the Essex to Munich Trench. Martineau, the Brigade Signalling Officer, went off to raise a forward signal station, which he did somewhere on 63. Over and over again we got the message back from him saying that the Essex were bombing in Munich Trench and wanted more bombs. Of the King's Own we never heard a word, apart from the Adjutant who came into headquarters with a cracked head. This was the first action in which steel helmets were worn and they undoubtedly saved many lives.

Just before the Brigade went over, the Division ordered us to stop the battalions, and also stop 10 Brigade. Runners were immediately sent to the King's Own, Essex, Lancashire Fus and Dukes.

Captain A Weatherhead, King's Own (Royal Lancaster Regiment). Killed 1 July, his body was never identified. He is commemorated on the Thiepval Memorial.

They were too late however. The King's Own and the Essex were right on. The Lancashire Fus were mostly in the Quadrilateral and one company of the Dukes was in the Bosch line.

The result of all this was that 93 Brigade, having failed on the left and the 29th Division on the right, the Germans came down from either flank and the King's Own and Essex were practically missing. Major Bromilow has not been heard of since. Colonel Stirling, the CO of the Essex, was wounded twice at the beginning and got taken away. Caddick, the Adjutant of the Essex, and the adjutant of the King's Own were both wounded.

The 2/Seaforths had already sent out patrols, led by Lieutenant Harrison, who was immediately hit and badly wounded. They attacked at the same time as the Dublins, too soon to get the message and, initially, fire from the redoubt forced many men to move about 150 yards to the south, before the guns were silenced by patrols of the Scottish soldiers who attacked Ridge Redoubt. Meanwhile, the remainder of the battalion were drawn towards the Quadrilateral by veering sharply to the left of Ridge Redoubt, and thereby avoiding some of the worst firepower on the right. Many joined up with those of the Rifle Brigade and the Somersets in Beaumont Trench, and as they approached, were seen by these occupants who cheered and shouted encouragement to their colleagues. This startled the Seaforths who initially stopped and took cover thinking it was the Germans up front who were jeering at their predicament. They succeeded in stopping right in the middle of the German barrage and were heavily shelled, taking many casualties before the mistake was recognized. The group that had attacked the redoubt carried on after knocking out the machine guns, but veering sharply to the left. They crossed Beaumont Trench

The Seaforths' roll call after the battle...

and continued almost parallel to Munich Trench. They eventually crossed it near where it joined Wagon road under cover of the right hand bank of a valley that carried the trench known as Ten Tree Alley. Here they were able to join some troops of the King's Own and Dukes who had got through on the left of the attack.

Brigadier General Prowse was the commanding officer of the 11 Brigade and was anxious to get forward to see for himself what was happening. So many commanding officers and their adjutants were casualties that information was very scarce. His last message from headquarters was timed at 8.50am saying that he was advancing, that is fifteen minutes after the messages were sent with the intention of holding up the second assault. In taking his brigade headquarters

forward, he would have been caught up in the advance of 12 Brigade and according to an eye witness, Lieutenant Hawkins of the 2/Lancashire Fusiliers, joined in the attack.

General Prowse left the Headquarters too soon and was killed rushing a machine gun. He was shot in the stomach and died at Marieux, Corps Headquarters, that evening.

On the left of the second assault, the 2/Essex and the 1/King's Own suffered heavy casualties from shell fire even before crossing the British front line at 9.30am. The commanding officers and adjutants were both casualties Major Bromilow (King's) was killed, and Lieutenant Colonel Sir George Stirling (Essex) severely wounded and information and reports were very scarce. At one point two small mines were exploded under the King's. German fire was especially heavy on the left, from Serre and it was the right companies that got through and into the German front line. Units of both

...near the same place today. Note the bumpy track along which Lieutenant Shearn and many others were wheeled, to the site of the old sucrerie on the skyline which was near the trees.

battalions supported the Warwicks in between the German front line and Beaumont Trench. Some even managed to join the group that passed the *Feste Soden*, advanced towards Frankfurt Trench and then, crossing Ten Tree Alley, a long and substantial communication trench, were seen approaching Pendant Copse. Reports as to the size of this group vary, from a few to several hundred. Two British aircraft bravely flew at very low level up and down the lines and it was from one of these that the reports of a breakthrough emanated. Because of the poor visibility, due to smoke and dust, several hundred men in a limited location could well have been mistaken as a breakthrough, and so I favour the idea that a substantial number of men from mixed units, including some from the 31st 'Pals' Division, got through.

There remains just three of the fourteen battalions which attacked that day as the 4th Division to account for. The 2/Lancashire Fusiliers only attacked with half a battalion, that is two companies, and they went forward with the second assault. Some of their number also got through into the area of the Quadrilateral, which was becoming exceedingly crowded and uncomfortable. Lieutenant Hawkins continued:

> Fighting went on all the afternoon. Some of the Seaforths of the 10 Brigade got over and joined up with the Lancs. Fus in the Quadrilateral. The CO of the Seaforths, Hodge, Bertie Ravenscroft, Hall, Watkins, Mansell, and Rougier were in the Quad with him and stayed there till 2am. July 2nd, bombing the whole time. CSM Laverick and Sgt Albon were there too. These two found a Stokes gun and although they had never seen one before worked it till they ran dry of ammunition. B. Farrow was killed in No Man's Land on his way back having been with the others all the time. The Roman Road (Watling Street) on the afternoon of July 1st was ghastly, wounded in every place conceivable coming up all the time. MacDonald with a bullet in his chest and a Bosche helmet was the only one of the officers I saw from the Regt. He was quite happy.

The 1/Royal Irish were held back from the second assault but, later in the day, two companies were sent forward to reinforce and relieve those in the Quadrilateral where Lieutenant Colonel J O Hopkinson of the Seaforth Highlanders was holding out. Captain Wilson with A Company failed to get through, and the officer was a casualty. Captain Barefoot leading D Company got there by a circuitous route and at 8.30pm was ordered to hold his position at all costs. During the night three separate messages were sent to Barefoot ordering him to

Exhausted and dejected men of the Lancashire Fusiliers tend to the wounded in a trench near the White City.

withdraw, but none got through. Eventually, at 10.30 am on 2 July, a message got through and the position was abandoned. The men of the Royal Irish Rifles had held on for eighteen hours with the remnants of the occupants of the previous days fighting. The last battalion, the 1/Royal Warwicks, were never brought forward into the fight, being ordered to halt behind the 2/Royal Dublin Fusiliers. A strong patrol, though, was sent out on the south side of Ridge Redoubt at 1.30 pm. A Company, led by Lieutenant Waters, went to make a reconnaissance. It went as far as Watling Street before being stopped by machine gun fire. The battalion held the front line on the night of 1/2 July.

We can now return to Lieutenant Glover of the 1/Rifle Brigade in Beaumont Trench, who was under counter attack from the Germans. It was about 11.00 am when the Germans launched their attack on the men in Beaumont Trench and the trenches behind in the Quadrilateral.

We were attacked by the German bombers and resisted them falling back slightly, then they seemed to work round to our right rear. However, we kept a look out on that side and a Lewis gun on the parapet of a communication trench running back dominated the open. Captain Martin of the 8th Warwicks kept the

Scenes typical of those at the Sucrerie.

men busy as well as he could at strengthening our left, but it was hard work, the men seemed dazed and careless.

Men from all units were driven back by heavy bombing attacks from both the right and left flanks and suddenly Glover noticed that there were Germans behind him in a communication trench. It was very crowded.

We managed by scraping shallow trenches to get in some men from the shell holes beyond. Others came in over the top – or didn't. Gradually our bit of trench filled up with a great many of the 12th Brigade and some of the 10th. We were a fearful squash in the trench and it was extremely difficult to move or dig. I did try, but not very successfully, to spread out the 11th to the right and Captain Martin also tried to get the 10th and 12th to the left, but they were held back and couldn't get along the single trench. Suddenly our right was rushed by the Germans and the men next to our battalion bombing squad rushed back and our bombing squad was cut off.

Sergeant Cook of the 1/Somersets continues the story:

Colonel Hopkinson of the Seaforths was doing excellent work, he seemed to be the only officer here, and was seen walking around the Quadrilateral giving encouragement to all. He saved a dangerous situation; someone gave an order to retire, there was an immediate panic, and some four to five hundred retired, in spite of great efforts to stem the rush by the Colonel and us sergeants present. The Colonel then ordered a bugler of the Seaforths to sound the "charge"; this had the immediate effect and saved the situation.

Number 68 Drummer Ritchie, 2/Seaforth Highlanders, repeatedly jumped out of the occupied German trenches and sounded the "Charge" in an attempt to stop men from falling back, walking up and down, out in the open and exposing himself to great danger. By some miracle he was not hit, and later he was to be awarded the Victoria Cross.

Sergeant A H Cook, 1/Somersets, survived the war and became a 'Beefeater' at the Tower of London.

The men with Glover were surrounded but gathered all the bombs they could and fought a rearguard action for some hours. Four throwers, especially, did excellent work. They were supplied, for the main part, by one man who retrieved bombs from various previously abandoned positions. He was the runner of the commanding officer of the 8/Warwicks,

This runner made the trip between that trench and our own at

least twenty times, bringing bombs and L.G. ammunition. He did more than any individual to keep things going. Then towards 2pm or 3pm Trevor passed me up a note from the Colonel of the Seaforths to hold on, he would send some bombs. But for that runner even that would have come too late, the throwers were dog tired and the Germans full of energy. By persuasion we managed to get a team of about half a dozen who carried on manfully, some others would have done so had they not been wounded.

They held on until 4.30 pm when another German assault forced a retreat. However they secured their position with Lewis guns on the flanks and built barricades to prevent the Germans getting close enough to throw directly into their trench. For a long time the Germans threw into a vacant trench in front of Glover's men. The Germans behind them seemed to have disappeared. Glover heard an officer call to him from a dugout and while he was talking with him the end came with a rush. The Germans, who had been behind them, reappeared. They had managed to get into the vacant trench in front by crawling a circuitous route and were not seen by the Lewis gunners.

How they managed it, I don't know, possibly they had worked into a trench near our front, but the Germans suddenly threw bombs some of which fell on the traverse by the L.G. and drove our men out of the trench. An attempt to make a stand at the next traverse was unsuccessful. In the new trench, the front line, the base of the Quadrilateral, there seemed no definite plan. Then the Staff Captain turned up giving instructions to the CO of the Seaforths whom I now saw for the first time with a quantity of about 200 troops. He sent out of the trench all who were wounded including Trevor and myself.

(Lieutenant G W Glover was one of the few surviving officers of the 1/Rifle Brigade. He was awarded the DSO, but was killed in action on 18 August 1918.)

Meanwhile, Sergeant Cook was also involved in a rearguard action nearby:

The Germans were trying to force us out of their trenches. We got together what was left of us, and started collecting bombs from the dead and wounded, and then commenced a grenade battle in real earnest; but after two or three hours our supply of bombs ran out and there were no more to be got. The Germans then gradually drove us back inch by inch, through their superior supply of bombs. Again someone gave the order to "retire" and again men started to retire but we stopped this as every man was wanted in the trench. Our numbers were very small and men were being killed and wounded in all directions, it was difficult to walk in the trench without walking on the dead. Our troops were gradually retiring and only leaving a small garrison to hold the trench. It was very dangerous to move about, but bombs had to be got, so I went around and collected as many as I could find on the casualties. These were soon used up and now we had to retire to the former German front line, and try and hold out with rifle and machine guns, Jerry took advantage of the maze of

Bringing in the wounded in the 4th Division sector.

communication trenches to follow up every yard we gave. Our numbers were reduced to about fifty at this time. A second lieutenant of the Warwicks and I had a little pow-wow on the situation and decided to split the men we had equally between us and barricade the trench left and right and leave the open space between us to look after itself, so he went to the right and I to the left, until we gained contact with the enemy, then we made our barricade. I then got a few men to collect all bombs. A German commenced to approach us – I sniped him; but many followed with bombs and these now commenced another grenade contest, and the only bombs we had were the German stick bombs. We could see each other as the bombs were thrown, and we were actually throwing back the bombs they threw before they burst. The time fuse seemed much longer than our Mills bomb of four seconds. My numbers were becoming rapidly reduced, but we were holding our own until the enemy worked around to our right rear and began bombing us from this quarter. This was getting pretty hot but my orders were to hold on till midnight, when we were to be relieved, but we seemed to be the only British troops here, and my party now numbered nine. The trenches were full of German dead which we bombed out in the morning, and

41

we had to keep clambering backwards and forwards in our efforts to hold our own. Shells were now falling thick and fast, the enemy had apparently retired and asked for artillery support to try and dislodge us. We were relieved at 11 pm and ordered to go back. I saw Sergeant Imber at the end of a German sap. I said, "Come on Sam, we are relieved" Sam had about six German helmets hung on him. We started off and Jerry dropped a barrage on No Man's Land, and what with the blinding flash of shells, barbed wire and shell holes, we soon lost each other. How I escaped I do not know. I tripped over dead bodies, fell headlong into shell holes, my clothes were torn to ribbons by barbed wire. I lost sense of direction and eventually fell sprawling, dead beat to the world. As soon as I recovered I saw a form standing over me with a fixed bayonet. He thought I was a German and I thought he was; but thank God it was a British sentry. He had received orders that no British troops were in front, so I nearly got shot by our own men after being out there since 7.30 am. At roll call no officer who went into action (there were 26) was present, 17 were killed, 1 captured and 8 wounded. All warrant officers were killed, 7 sergeants survived, I was fortunately one of those.

So the Quadrilateral was given up except for the original German front line. That, too, was finally abandoned. There had been nearly 6,000 casualties and many of those wounded laid out in No Man's Land.

We return to complete the story of Lieutenant Shearn of the 1/Hampshires, who we left lying in Watling Street, who recalled:

Coming back to myself roughly bandaged and in the sunken road (Watling Street)*, I have no memory of much pain. I had in my haversack a first aid outfit which contained a bottle of chloroform and morphine in liquid form – pale green I think it was. The dose was six drops so far as I remember. I accordingly poured six drops of my mixture and licked them off. I reflected that probably I would not thus get the benefit of the full six drops, some would stick to my hand. I accordingly gave myself another three drops for luck. Nothing very much happened so I repeated the proceedings later on. I think eventually I had swigged the whole bottleful. I don't think I went to sleep but I may have. I don't remember seeing any of the Seaforths going through though I heard they did attack and a few penetrated the German front line. I remember Tommy Fawkes coming back well primed – probably from the rum ration – and sitting on top of the bank* *of the sunken road. He chatted for a bit despite the obvious danger of his position, then quite cheerily he remarked "Well, I must be going" and pushed off. I raised my voice and called for stretcher bearers. Someone came along and I remember a voice saying "Blimey, it's an officer". After a considerable length of time they got me to the place where our medical officer was conducting operations. This was in dead ground and was comparatively safe* (White City). *I stayed in the dug-out for quite a while and when it was dark I was put in my stretcher on some two-wheeled contraption for carrying stretchers. I was wheeled over some pretty broken ground and dumped on the side of the road opposite a ruined "sucrerie". I didn't care for this much as I knew the Germans shelled this road from time to time. Eventually my stretcher and those alongside were loaded onto motor ambulances.*

Lieutenant E D Shearn survived his wounds and returned to his battalion and was promoted to captain. He later joined the Royal Flying Corps and was a Flying Officer. He took part in the 60th commemoration of the Somme battles in 1976.

Work continued over the next few days, mainly at night, bringing in the wounded, but it was beyond the resources of the stretcher bearers and the medics to make much progress. It was reported that the German soldiers were out in No Man's Land on 2 July burying the dead near their front line.

Lieutenant Colonel Fitzgerald of the Royal Army Medical Corps was attached to the 1/Royal Irish Fusiliers. He had been working to bring in the wounded and on 5 July arranged for a large Red Cross banner to be made. At 4.00 pm it was hoisted above the British trenches. Normally, any movement would have been met by a burst of machine gun fire, but this time nothing happened. Some time elapsed after which Fitzgerald climbed up out of the trench and showed himself to the enemy. Another officer joined him and the banner was carried forward into No Man's Land. In the German trenches an officer got out and walked towards the them. He was wearing a Red Cross brassard on his arm and a white handkerchief was tied to a walking stick. They approached each other and halted at a distance and saluted. The German officer gestured around him at all the dead and wounded. He beckoned forward German soldiers from their trenches who emerged and began carrying the wounded over to the British side of No Man's Land, where they were met by British soldiers who continued the process until they reached the British trenches. This work continued until 11.00 pm when it was too dark to see any more or all the wounded had been retrieved. Not a word was said between the two officers during this time who finally saluted each other again and returned to their respective trenches. Almost immediately a German barrage opened up on the British lines.

The following information indicates that the officer whose actions are recorded here was probably Lieutenant Colonel G Fitzgerald, Royal Army Medical Corps, DSO and Bar. He was born 29 May 1878 and educated at the Royal College of Surgeons of Ireland in Dublin, and also at the Rotunda Hospital. He joined the army in April 1900 with the rank of lieutenant. He was promoted to captain in1903 and major in January 1912. He was on active service immediately the war broke out and was in the retreat from Mons. By the beginning of 1916 he was promoted to lieutenant colonel. He was twice mentioned in despatches and was awarded the first of his DSOs on 1 January 1917 'for distinguished service in the field'. On 27 July 1918 he was awarded the second DSO 'for conspicuous gallantry and devotion to duty. When his casualty clearing station was shelled he not only evacuated his patients to places of safety, but salved practically all the stores of his unit. This action was performed twice over, and on both occasions his courage and ability were pre-eminent.'

Lieutenant Hawkins wrote in the Brigade Diary:

The Bosch showed his fighting powers that day, and he put up a grand fight. It was, however, nearly all his officers. The machine guns in our vicinity were nearly all manned by Bosch officers and all the prisoners told us the same. The prisoners, numbering fifteen, were all Wurttenburgers.

The Bosch had put up a very fine barrage of 5.9 HE and shrapnel. He put up every gun in a clump on to one small bit of front, using his machine guns elsewhere. After ten minutes he would shift all his guns to another small portion of the front and so on, always having a machine gun barrage where his guns were not firing. It was most effective. He also blew a couple of mines in No Man's Land under out first wave.

CHAPTER TWO

THE NOVEMBER BATTLES
MONDAY 13 NOVEMBER

It was to be November before any further attack was launched in earnest north of the river Ancre. True, an attack on 3 September astride the river Ancre was made by the 39th Division on the north bank and 49th Division on the south bank, to support the left flank of the 18th Division, whose task was the main prize, the Thiepval Ridge.

The 49th Division failed where, previously, the 36th Ulster Division also had to give second best, but not before driving all before them in a glorious and heroic charge that only narrowly failed for lack of support. The hard pressed Germans frantically threw reinforcements forward to hold on to the village of Grandcourt and regain the Schwaben Redoubt which had been overrun. In September, the tired and inexperienced Yorkshiremen never had any chance of success but were criticised for being apathetic and lacking in determination for their trouble.

Similarly, on the north bank of the Ancre, the 39th Division, with some battalions less than half strength, and without adequate support or reserve, broke against strongly defended lines. These lines were later to frustrate and decimate the battalions of the Royal Naval Division, before being overcome with the assistance of the tanks. All that apart, the area around the village of Beaumont Hamel and across

British troops attack, September 1916.

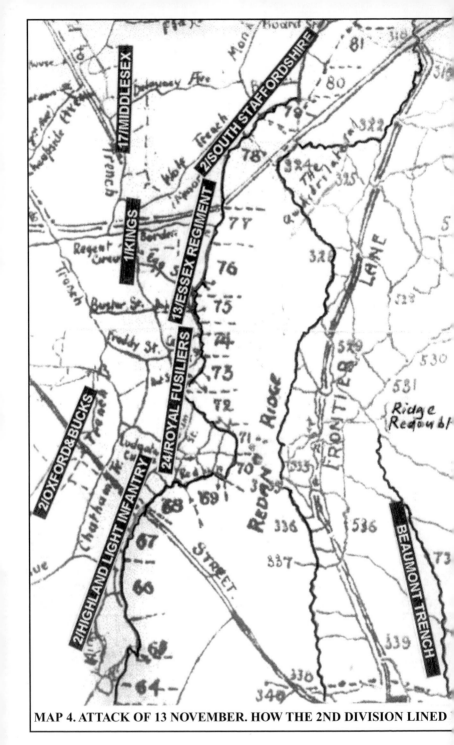

MAP 4. ATTACK OF 13 NOVEMBER. HOW THE 2ND DIVISION LINED

Redan Ridge to Serre remained 'quiet' and no major offensive took place.

The battles that commenced in November had originally been intended to take place on 23 September, but bad weather had set in. The end of September brought a series of cancellations. The beginning of October heralded a period that produced rain of varying amounts on no less than twenty one days until 9 November, when the frost arrived. A report for the following day, 10 November, simply stated; *'Mud prevented any movement'*.

The window in the weather provided the first opportunity to make the assault and General Gough, commanding the Fifth Army, prepared orders to attack on 13 November.

Men were falling sick because of exposure to the conditions and numbers in the ranks were slowly being

Lieutenant Frank Goldsmith Adjutant of the 14/Hampshire (39th Division) in September 1916, went on to command the battalion, but was later killed in action.

eroded. Sir Douglas Haig became very concerned about the situation and on 12 November went to Fifth Army headquarters at Toutencourt to discuss the situation with General Gough. Haig was of the opinion that the attack ought to be called off, as the conditions, surely, would limit the chances of success and he did not want another failure. Gough, though, was of the opinion that there was a realistic chance, and if the opportunity was not taken now, then within another few days the state of the men would render an attack impossible altogether. Haig, realised that any success at the onset of winter on the Western front would have valuable repercussions on the Eastern front, and Germany might have to transfer troops from that arena to bolster their effort here and this would be a major achievement for the British. Reluctantly, Haig changed his mind and allowed Gough to proceed.

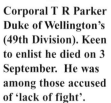

Corporal T R Parker Duke of Wellington's (49th Division). Keen to enlist he died on 3 September. He was among those accused of 'lack of fight'.

The task of capturing Redan Ridge and moving across the ridges to the north-east of the village towards Munich Trench and Frankfurt Trench was allotted to the battalions of the 2nd Division,

General Sir Hubert Gough, commander of the Fifth Army.

commanded by Major General W G Walker. 5 and 6 Brigades were to lead the attack on a four battalion front with the 2/Highland Light Infantry (5 Brigade) on the extreme right and on the divisional boundary with the 51st (Highland) Division. Next on their left was the 24/Royal Fusiliers, while in 6 Brigade sector on the right was the 13/Essex, and on the extreme left of the sector, next to the troops of the 3rd Division, was the 2/South Staffordshire Regiment. The battalions in support, reading as before, from right to left, were 17/Royal Fusiliers, 2/Oxfordshire and Buckinghamshire Light Infantry, 1/King's and the 17/Middlesex Regiment. Four Lewis guns and four guns of the 6 Brigade Machine Gun Company supported the front line troops of each battalion.

In the opposite trenches, the German troops were drawn from the 12 Division, the 23 Regiment, and Battalions I and III were in the line.

On the night of 11 November patrols had gone out and reported back that No Man's Land was in a terrible condition. The mud was very deep and there was a profusion of shell holes and larger craters that had filled up with water. Each man making the crossing carried 150 rounds of small arms ammunition (SAA), in addition they had two Mills bombs, two sandbags, one iron ration and one day's ration in addition to the ration issued for that day. Twenty men from each company (about eighty in all) took picks and shovels. To assist observation, a piece of red material was attached to everyone's back.

On preceding days a barrage had opened at 5.00 am after which nothing occurred, and this duly took place in an attempt to deceive the enemy. However, this time at 5.45 am all the 18-pounders and the trench mortar batteries joined in. In a repeat performance of events on 1 July, the nearby Hawthorn Crater was blown again, on this occasion at the exact time the main barrage opened and the troops, many of whom were lying out in No Man's Land, because the trenches were filled with mud, commenced their advance. The charge consisted of 30,000 pounds of ammonal and it almost completely destroyed its occupants, about 350 men, only sixty surviving, who were soon taken prisoner. Another much smaller mine was blown in 5 Brigade sector opposite a trench named Cat Street. It was still quite dark and there was a thick mist but the men of the 2/Highland LI and the 24/Royal Fusiliers were successful and managed to keep up behind the British barrage. The 2/Highland Light Infantry (LI) were led by Captain Watkyn-Thomas (B Company) and Captain Austin Cartmell (two platoons of D Company). Some men played their mouth organs as they went across, making good progress but getting too close to the barrage in places, incurring some casualties. In about six minutes, even only proceeding at a walk, the first parties arrived at the German front line while the barrage was still on it and further casualties occurred.

Large sections of the wire had been destroyed and the Germans seemed to have been taken by surprise and about 150 were captured from the front line garrison as they emerged from their dugouts. The second wave of the 2/Highland LI was led by Captain Richardson (the two remaining platoons of D Company). Finally, the consolidation was left to A company and the battalion machine-gun crews. The Germans in their second and third lines, though, were now alerted and as the men of both the HLI and the Royal Fusiliers pressed on towards Beaumont Trench they took many casualties from machine gun fire. Snipers were very active, although visibility was less than thirty yards as the dawn broke. In the event, though, elements of men from the two battalions arrived at the first objective and they were on time. Further prisoners had been taken, the 2/Highland LI alone accounting for 207 unwounded men and fair quantities of war material.

As the first assault took place, so it was followed up by the advance of 17/Royal Fusiliers and the 2/Ox & Bucks who were to 'leap-frog' the men in Beaumont Trench and push on to Frankfurt Trench. Little is known of their progress, except that both battalions lost direction in the fog and veered to the left and were actually travelling parallel to the direction of the attack. They arrived at a communication trench named Lager Alley, where the mistake was discovered. This position was inside 6 Brigade sector and close to the rear of the Quadrilateral. Both

Germans under bombardment rush to man the trenches.

units were now completely mixed up and composite groups, which included a few men from the Essex and King's, attempted to advance towards the second objective, the Serre-Beaucourt road and Frankfurt Trench. The total force only numbered about 120. The timing of this advance was originally intended to be at 7.30 am but it is not clear when they actually went forward. Heavy fighting ensued at Munich Trench where the German 23 Regiment were in the line. Some groups of the Ox and Bucks men got through and advanced as far as Frankfurt Trench. Two companies of the second battalion of the German regiment were sufficient to repel the remainder, although had the numbers of their attackers been greater they had no available reinforcements to call on. The Ox and Bucks men found themselves isolated and those that were able to made a retirement. Some other small and isolated units of the 17/Royal Fusiliers also succeeded in getting to Frankfurt Trench further south, but they too, being isolated, returned to Wagon road and then to Beaumont Trench. As we will see, 6 Brigade was in difficulties and men of the Ox and Bucks were

Attempting to bail out a flooded trench on the Somme.

employed to form a defensive flank at the junctions of Lager Alley, Beaumont Trench and Serre Trench, on the left of the brigade sector, which was very unstable and under attack. Further south, or on the right of the sector, the 17/Royal Fusiliers reinforced the northern end of Beaumont Trench, as far as the junction with Crater Lane, which itself was occupied as far as Wagon Road and where observation posts were established on the high banking close to Beaumont village. The time was about 10.00 am and contact was established with the 51st Highland Division, who were in the village.

Meanwhile, things did not go as well in 6 Brigade sector on the left. On the left of the sector, where it conjoined with the 3rd Division who were attacking Serre village, the 2/South Staffs, in the fog and darkness, were guided forward by their officers on compass bearings. They were followed by the 17/Middlesex. Although progress was slow through the mud, the German front line was reached and taken, the main casualties being as a result of the left company getting too close to their own barrage. The time was then 6.30 am. Thereafter disaster struck.

Troops of two battalions of the Royal Scottish Fusiliers from the neighbouring 3rd Division completely lost direction moving sharply to the right, and became hopelessly mixed up with the South Staffs men who themselves had also veered off course, somewhat to the left. Furthermore, by that time the attack on Serre had been deemed a failure and attempts were being made to recover the men who had been defeated as much by the conditions as anything. Men were seen to be half buried up to the waist and it was here the mud was at its worst. So while the Staffordshire men were still trying to get forward the Scots were trying to get back. The retiring men then became entangled with the 17/Middlesex who were in Fargate Trench, still in the British lines. By now the barrage had moved on and the men of 6 Brigade were exposed to the German counter attack. A barrage was opened up and a storm of machine gun fire swept in enfilade from the direction of Serre, whose defenders now found themselves free from direct attack. More enfilade fire came from the right where, as we shall see, the other half of the brigade had stalled in front of the Quadrilateral. There was an acute shortage of bombs, the meagre ration soon being expended. Rifles were clogged with mud and would not fire, the only weapon left was the bayonet, if only they could get close enough to the Germans! Some valiant efforts were made to get through the mostly intact wire. One lieutenant got some way down Ten Tree Alley, before being held up and then wounded before returning. There was nothing left to do but to withdraw to the British front line.

The last two battalions of 6 Brigade, the 13/Essex, followed by the 1/King's, had the Quadrilateral opposite their positions. This, it will be recalled, was the scene of costly fighting on 1 July. The men got away promptly, following the barrage. Thereafter nothing was seen or heard of them. At 7.45 am, that is fifteen minutes after the assault on Frankfurt trench was intended to commence from Beaucourt Trench, Lieutenant Colonel Carter, commanding the 13 Essex, sent out a four man patrol to see what had happened. They reported that nothing could be seen of the right companies but some of the left were near the German front line, sheltering under the roadside embankment.

Captain C G Carson, 13th Essex Regiment, led C Company gallantly and was severely wounded. He remained at his post with his men. He died of his wounds at Rouen 19 November. He was awarded the Military Cross.

It transpired that the right companies had forced a way through, finding a way to the right of the Quadrilateral from which direction a few bombs were thrown but little else, the machine guns, as we have seen, were concentrated in the other direction:

We pushed forward, over the second and third German lines, and arrived at the Green Line [Beaumont Trench] *a few minutes after our own artillery barrage had lifted. I found myself with two Lewis gun teams and sixty men and the signalling officer; also one Lewis gun team and a few men of the King's (Liverpool) Regiment with an officer of the 2nd South Staffords Regiment. On looking round my position I found that the left flank was exposed, owing to the remainder of the waves not reaching their objective. I immediately placed two Lewis guns on this flank and commenced consolidating this position. A small party of the enemy attempted to bomb us, but were dispersed by Lewis gunfire. I next visited the third line, and found that the junction of Lager Alley was a weak point, so I placed my third Lewis gun at this point.*

So, by midday, little had been gained by 6 Brigade except an isolated 'toe hold' in Beaumont Trench and work started immediately to consolidate this position by constructing a trench from here back to the original British front line. The men who were left from the scattered battalions were then gathered together back in the British front line and were reorganised into two composite battalions. On the left men of the

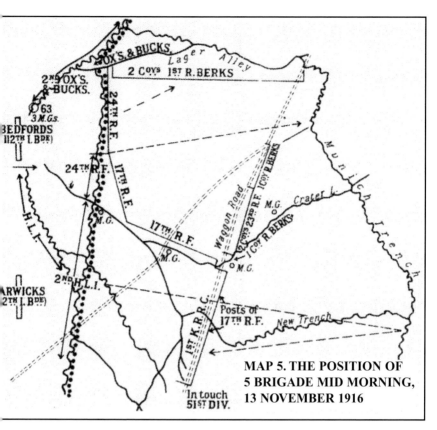

MAP 5. THE POSITION OF
5 BRIGADE MID MORNING,
13 NOVEMBER 1916

1/King's, 2/South Staffs and 17/Middlesex, numbered about 300; while on the right more of the 1/King's and the 13/Essex amounted to 250. Only these remained from an original force in excess of about 2,500, less, of course those holding out in Beaumont Trench.

An order for a renewed attack in the afternoon was received from V Corps Headquarters. 6 Brigade were in no fit state, and reinforcements from the Division's remaining 99 Brigade were sent forward. This attack was to be in conjunction with another assault by the 3rd Division at Serre. The bombardment was already in progress and the 22/Royal Fusiliers (99 Brigade) had moved into position when the attack was cancelled; the 3rd Division being unable to co-operate because of the losses it had sustained. Further verbal orders were then given for 99 Brigade to attack Munich Trench; but this too was cancelled and it was decided to mount this operation on the morning of 14 November.

Tuesday 14 November

In preparation for the attack the 22/Royal Fusiliers were moved to the brigade boundary on the left where it met with 6 Brigade sector. This was close to the Quadrilateral and also near to where the Ox and Bucks men were still positioned. Machine guns and snipers were still active in the heart of the redoubt and would pose a serious threat to the flank of the proposed attack on Munich Trench. Lieutenant Gell led A Company but he was shot in the knee and Second Lieutenant Kelly took over. He found a strongpoint built by the Essex on his right and established his troops to the left inside the salient of the redoubt. B Company, who were to follow up and extend the line further to the left towards the old British front line, got lost and returned to their starting point. It was very dark, misty and the ground was very boggy, but D Company, in turn, set out and found the position and completed the defensive flank to the left back as far as the old line. A strongpoint was then built right in the centre of the Quadrilateral and another in the southern face of the salient.

While this operation was completed, the attack was launched from Beaucourt Trench at 6.20 am. On the right, nearest Beaumont Hamel village, the 1/King's Royal Rifle Corps were on a two company front and, on their left, the 1/Royal Berkshire were similarly established. Behind them, a company of the 23/Royal Fusiliers were in support to

A German sniper in action.

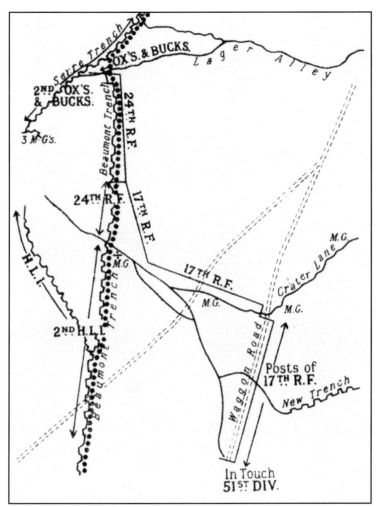

MAP 6. THE NIGHT OF 13/14 NOVEMBER.

the Royal Berks left flank and a similar arrangement was made to support the left of the King's Royal Rifle Corps. Once again the proceedings were shrouded in dense fog. Between four and a half and five hours were allowed to get the men from the old British front line into Beaumont Trench, the jumping off point, a distance at the maximum of half a mile. However, only one company of the KRRC arrived at the start line, with just four minutes to go before zero. There was no time for any preparation and the result was something near chaos. The intense difficulties of forming up in the conditions soon gave way to even deeper mud, shell holes full of water, tangled wire

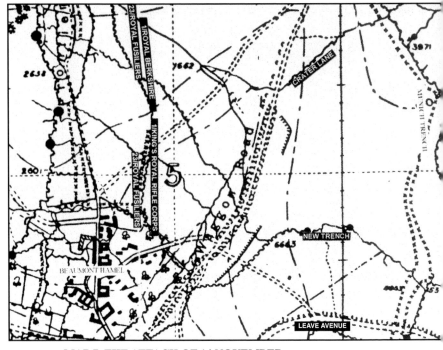

MAP 7. THE ATTACK OF 14 NOVEMBER.

and the German trenches hardly distinguishable, full of muddy water and slime. At 6.30 am two advances were made on the right. Four officers and eighty men arrived at Leave Avenue, which was in the 51st Division sector, and began consolidating under the impression it was Munich Trench. It was, in fact, a communication trench running forward towards the objective which was still eighty yards distant. When the mistake was discovered, bombers were sent forward to attack Munich Trench but they were hampered by their own barrage which was still falling on their objective. They were also caught by heavy sniper fire. Being isolated, and with no contact either on the left or the right, the attempt was abandoned, but

Second Lieutenant G C Stoneham 1/ Royal Berks. Killed 14 November and is buried in Munich Trench British Cemetery.

not without some issue as the occupants of Leave Avenue, two German officers and sixty other ranks were taken prisoner. The time was 1.30 pm.

Meanwhile, on the left, the other half of the KRRC attack was made on New Trench, another communication trench leading into Munich Trench. There were two groups and the first group got to within

56

30 yards of Munich Trench, while the other mistook New Trench for Munich Trench. They were, in fact, still 150 yards short of their objective and, realising their error, an attack was organised from shell holes in No Man's Land. The British barrage was still falling, however, and no progress could be made and the men were ordered to dig in. As daylight broke it became apparent that they were entirely cut off and isolated, and in direct enfilade from German snipers. An order was given to retire down New Trench and by 9.30 am all those able had returned to Wagon road. Of the young officers ordered to lead this hopeless mission the KRRC lost four killed in action, Lieutenant The Hon. F S Trench, Lieutenant J H T Liddell by shell fire and Second Lieutenants T U Roydan and R F Lowndes were seen to be shot down while courageously standing up to direct the fire of their men. Three others were wounded. Seventeen other ranks were killed, thirteen were missing and 109 wounded.

Lieutenant A A S Hamilton, 1/Royal Berks. Evauated from the battlefield but died at Etaples awaiting evacuation to England.

In the meantime the 1/Royal Berks moved off but, on the right of the attack, were far too close to the British barrage. It was later disputed whether the barrage was short or the men too far ahead, but the outcome was the same and they lost 116 out of 159 on the way across. A further group of about fifteen men became separated and the result was that only ten to fifteen men of the leading wave arrived in front of Munich Trench. They were led by two officers, Second Lieutenants E D D'O Astley and G C Stoneham. Undeterred, they got through the wire and jumped into the trench. Almost immediately Lieutenant Stoneham was shot dead. Lieutenant Astley and his few gallant comrades pressed on and some German soldiers coming out of their dugouts threw their hands up and surrendered when they saw the British soldiers. Astley then went off to look for any other Royal Berks men, but finding none returned to where the prisoners were being held. By then the British barrage had lifted and the Germans began to emerge from their dugouts in numbers and attack the invaders, who got out of the trench and fell back about thirty yards and took cover in some shell holes, with the intention of attacking again. Just then two German officers and about fifty men got out of Munich Trench and, holding their hands up, shouted 'Kamerade' gave themselves up to the Berkshire men.

Almost immediately large numbers of Germans began to man the

PRIVATE T H PHILPOT

Private T H Philpot, 23/Royal Fusiliers killed in action on 14 November, wrote his last letter home in his dugout by the light of a candle five days before his death.

I am quite well in myself, but am not so strong as when I came out. Even only after three months out here one cannot be as fit as before. We often get wet through, and now the trenches are so wet and muddy it is impossible to keep the feet and legs dry. The second time I went into the trenches we were walking about in water up to our knees. When in the trenches on night post duty the cardigan, tunic, jerkin, great coat, equipment, and mackintosh cape are worn. By the time we have it all on we are some size but standing still watching for an hour at a time is cold work...We generally get a bath the day after we come out of the trenches, it is very seldom we are able to wash at all in the lines. You ought to see me after four days without a shave! Socks are the only articles of clothing we get short in. They get wet and muddy and after being rinsed out in cold water one or twice are not much good... When we are in the trenches the food is sent up in sand bags and we do our own cooking. That is where the fun comes in...This battalion has been out for just a year and with the exception of a few NCOs no leave has been granted. From this you can calculate I shall be due for leave... I must thank you for kindly sending all the parcels... I should like any cigarettes sent in tins... a tin stands the water better... I should like a few more candles. We have some issued and are able to buy them, but we have to light up early now when in the trenches, and I like to keep a light going in the dugout all night. This is the only way to keep the rats away. They are absolutely fearless. You can shout and make a noise, but they take no notice. They are born within the sound of guns. A light keeps them off, but when you put it out you can hear them sniffing like dogs. They bite through our haversacks to get at our rations. I have had two new haversacks since I came out.

Thomas Philpot was the son of Councillor and J. P. Mr T Philpot and his wife, of Ilford. He was clerk to the govenors of Ilford County High School. He is buried in Redan Ridge Cemetery No 1.

parapet of Munich Trench and a counterattack was launched down the communication trench known as Crater Lane under cover of heavy frontal and enfilade fire. Lieutenant Astley, who was the only remaining officer from the two companies of the Berkshires who assaulted on the right, gathered together what men he could find and fell back to Crater Lane near to its junction with Wagon road, where they built a block to prevent any further German progress.

Meanwhile, the two left companies moved forward with their extreme left forming a defensive flank on Lager Alley, where it joined with the positions established and held by the 22/Royal Fusiliers close to the Quadrilateral. In the fog and darkness and possibly because the left flank was facing in the wrong direction to Munich Trench, the whole attack veered further to the left and the men were actually travelling at a right angle along No Man's Land towards the 3rd Division sector. Lager Alley was totally destroyed and unrecognizable and the 'advance' continued crossing into German territory until Serre trench was reached, which was in the neighbouring division's sector. Here, too, the trench was badly smashed, and a sector was taken. The German defenders must have been surprised to see British infantry emerging through the fog from the rear! There were still some good dugouts intact and in one of them were found a number of 1/KRRC wounded prisoners being tended by a German doctor and fifty other ranks. Eventually all troops involved in the attack were withdrawn to Wagon road, where new positions were established. The 22/Royal Fusiliers extended their defensive flank to link with Wagon road.

At 2.45pm a second attempt was made to get to Frankfurt Trench and two battalions loaned from the 37th Division, 11/Royal Warwickshire and the 6/Bedfordshire, were sent forward. Meantime the damage caused by the British barrage had been considerable and there had been many German casualties. We have seen that many survivors were shaken and were content to surrender. The situation was critical in both Frankfurt and Munich trenches, there was a desperate lack of ammunition, bombs and supplies. Shellfire had destroyed the major source of drinking water, a well in Puisieux Trench, and many men had fallen ill drinking the foul water in the shell holes. All available men in the area were rushed forward to reinforce the Munich-Frankfurt position.

By the time the Warwicks and the Bedfords were ready to attack, the Germans had reorganized and were waiting for them. The men from the 37th Division had endured a long and tiring journey to the front. In addition, no one seems to have told them that the morning's attack on Munich Trench had failed and they were expecting to find that trench occupied by British troops, through whom they would pass. As soon as they advanced they were greeted by accurate and heavy machine-gun fire from the direction of Munich Trench and were unable to make any headway. Men soon began to fall back to Wagon road where there was now a large number of troops from different battalions sheltering.

That evening Sir Douglas Haig travelled to Paris to attend an inter-allied military conference. He received reports of the past two days events and proposed further attacks planned for Wednesday, 15 November, by V Corps. As a result of what he learnt he sent an order that no further attacks were to be undertaken until his return.

Same old trenches, same old view,
Same old rats as blooming tame,
Same old dugouts, nothing new,
Same old smells, the very same,
Same old bodies out in front,
Same old strafe from two till four,
Same old scratching, same old 'unt
Same old bloody war'

A A MILNE, (11/Warwickshire Regiment, fought on the Somme 1916).

A A Milne   Alan Alexander Milne was born in London on 18 January 1882 the son of a schoolmaster. He attended Westminster School and graduated from Cambridge University in 1902. He married in 1913 and lived in Chelsea. He wrote his first play, which was produced in London, after he joined the Royal Warwickshire Regiment on the outbreak of war. He fought in the July battles for the Bazentin Ridge and spent some time in Mametz Wood after its capture. As his battalion moved into the line for 14 November attack he became ill and as the assault took place was already on his way home to England. He arrived in Southampton on the 18th and never returned to the front, but remained in the Army on 'home' duties. He continued to write and became a fashionable London playwright with productions by 1919 in New York too. In 1920 Chistopher Robin Milne was born and this event changed the course of children's literature. The next few years saw the emergence of such books as *When We Were Young*, *Winnie-the-Pooh*, *The House at Pooh Corner* and *Now We Are Six*. Milne continued to write until his death in 1956.

CHAPTER THREE

WEDNESDAY 15 NOVEMBER

It was a November to be remembered with awe. The wind howled demonically. It rained. Sleet and snow drove across the dreary landscapes. The nights were gripped with frost. The melancholy Ancre merged its swollen puddles into a sluggish brown river, 300 yards wide at points. The battlefield bore resemblance to nothing on earth. Vast wildernesses of undulating mud through which stuck hedges of rusted barbed wire, blasted tree trunks, the remnants of broken and derelict defences. The trenches were crazy furrows in a mad ploughland, shallow, shapeless and slowly, slimily melting into the viscid ocean of mud. Men lay out in the shell holes, plastered like clay images, and, if the pelting sleet or the pelting shrapnel did not claim them they died of exhaustion and the slime oozed over them. Across the treacherous morasses troops moved on duckboards that sucked and slithered; for communication trenches were impossible. On these well marked and exposed routes the enemy batteries smashed down shells. It were better to die with a shard

Waiting for the assault.

of shell in the vitals than to slither maimed into the quagmires and die of gangrene or more surely by slow inches as the mud, the remorseless mud, crept up and over an enfeebled victim. Strong men, enduring soldiers, doomed to cross this wilderness with rations or signal messages, vanished without trace, shot down to disappear or too exhausted at the finish to combat the tentacles that seemed to rise from the mud to drag them down.

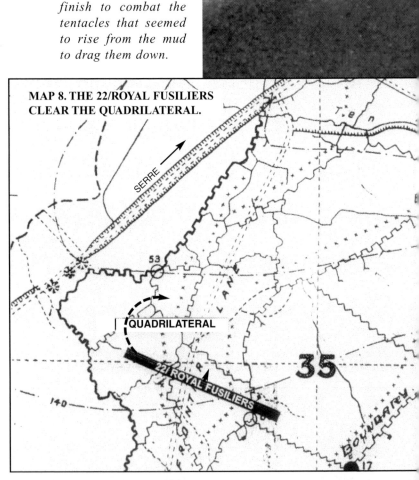

MAP 8. THE 22/ROYAL FUSILIERS CLEAR THE QUADRILATERAL.

German troops defend their positions with stick bombs.

During the night of 14, 15 November strenuous efforts were made to retrieve the wounded lying out in No Man's Land. Men from the artillery and mortar batteries were detailed to assist the Royal Army Medical Corps. The conditions for such work, it hardly needs to be said, could not have been worse. Neither did the Germans grant any favours and they remained on the alert for any movement that could possibly be a target in No Man's Land. Nevertheless, over two hundred severely wounded men had been carried back over hastily placed wooden trench boards which formed a causeway through the mud. Such was the effectiveness of this work that at one time there were over 100 wounded awaiting collection and return to Mailly Maillet (at the aid post in the White City). The RAMC lost twenty six men killed or wounded, including Lieutenant J B Stevenson and Captain W A Miller

DSO MC, medical officers of the 1/KRRC and the 22/Royal Fusiliers, respectively.

During the night some of the troops who had made the original assault on the morning of 13 November were relieved. They returned to the White City, en route to Mailly Maillet, bringing some of their wounded with them. Private Devine (2/HLI) was conspicuous in this work, making several journeys to bring in the wounded and was the last man away. During this period the 2/HLI had the misfortune to suffer a direct hit on their battalion headquarters at the White City. Among the casualties were Lieutenant Muir and Private Bullock, the latter a long serving battalion runner and a regular soldier.

Throughout the battle on 14 November, the Germans had tenaciously hung on to a portion of the Quadrilateral and resisted all attempts to dislodge them. In the early hours of the morning tanks were

MAP 9. 15 NOVEMBER. THE 10/LOYAL NORTH LANCASHIRE REGIMENT'S POSITION ON THE RIGHT BETWEEN LEAVE AVENUE AND CRATER LANE.

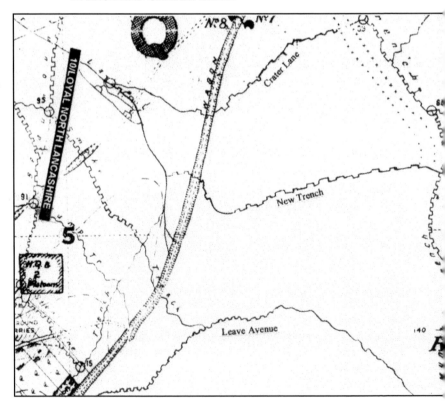

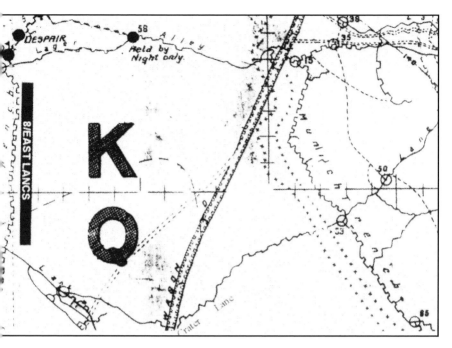

MAP 10. 15 NOVEMBER. THE POSITION OF THE LEFT OF THE ATTACK. THE 8/EAST LANCASHIRE FUSILIERS BETWEEN LAGER ALLEY AND CRATER LANE.

ordered forward, but they soon became stuck in the deep mud and never reached their destination. The lot of removing the Germans then fell to the 22/Royal Fusiliers. The attack commenced under a very heavy enemy barrage. Three bombing parties were detailed from A, B and D Companies. B Company worked through the German front line, bombing dugouts as they went and, meeting light opposition, made good progress forward. The other two companies were to work round through to the north side of the Quadrilateral and establish strong points on the higher ground. Their progress was slow because of near waist deep mud and the objective was only achieved with great difficulty. At one point a shell destroyed one of C Company's posts, but the men hung on bravely until the barrage abated at about 8.00 am. The Germans, seeing that their position was hopeless, and that their remaining portion of the Quadrilateral was entirely covered and overlooked by British gun crews, abandoned the fight and fell back in the direction of Munich Trench.

At 9.00 am, General Gough received a visit from Sir Douglas Haig's Chief of Staff, Lieutenant-General Kiggell, at Fifth Army Headquarters, telling him of Haig's decision. Gough, though,

William Frederick Ernest East

William East was the son of John East, a saddler and harness maker in Malvern, Worcester. He was the third eldest of six children. His main occupation was that of school teacher. However, he also worked as a musician, singer and entertainer. He was born in 1875 and was 41 when he died, leaving a wife and two children.

Will enlisted in the army during 1915 and was in France in the trenches by January 1916. Several of his postcards home and one of his letters have survived. By autumn 1916 he had been promoted to second lieutenant and was attached to the 8/East Lancashire Regiment.

William was killed in action on 15th November 1916 and is buried in Waggon Road Cemetery. Relatives still visit his grave.

subsequently 'lobbied' his divisional commanders and obtained their support to continue. Haig was still in Paris and Gough telephoned Kiggell at Querrieu and put his case. Kiggell travelled to Paris to see the Commander in Chief. After lengthy discussions Haig relented and for the second time in three days gave way against his better judgement. However, as we shall see, by the time all this had taken place, Gough was beginning to have doubts about his earlier optimism, which would, indeed, prove to be misplaced.

The remaining battalions of the 37th Division who, it will be recalled, had been loaned to the 2nd Division, were to be the beneficiaries of Gough's renewed attack. As early as 1.30 am the 8/East Lancs and the 10th Loyal North Lancs had begun to move forward from Mailly Maillet. Such was the difficulty in getting the men through the maze of trenches and broken and muddy ground that it was not until 7.45 am that the troops were finally in position in Beaumont Trench. The attack was due to commence at 8.30 pm. and Major General Walker, commanding, sent a message asking for a postponement until 1.00 pm. This was refused, however, and there was no time for any preparation or briefings. All that was known was that the objective, Munich Trench, lay to the front about 400 yards distant. The dispositions of the attack show that the 10/Loyal North Lancs were on the right, with troops of the 51st Division on their right flank and the 8/East Lancs were on the left, bordering the 3rd Division at Serre. The British barrage was very intense. A standing barrage was laid on the German trenches, while a moving barrage was to provide a curtain to protect the men as they followed it The advance was made on a two company front, again in very thick fog. Nothing seemed to happen for about 200 yards until the Germans realised that another attack was in progress. The barrage, though, was very erratic and many men began to fall, casualties of their own fire, rather than that of the Germans. The 8/East Lancs, who led with A and D Companies between Lager Alley and Crater Lane, then came under heavy rifle and machine-gun fire from their left. The advance came to a halt about fifty yards short of Munich Trench, where the wire was found to be mostly intact. Nevertheless, determined efforts were

Second Lieutenant R F Andrews 10/Loyal North Lancs. Killed 15 November and is buried in Frankfurt Trench Cemetery made by the officers to get into the trench, which was still being shelled by the British. Lieutenant Minnaar, alone, gallantly charged a machine gun position, but was shot dead. A platoon led by Lieutenant Jarintzoff managed to get into the trench and a number of Germans were killed, dugouts bombed and some prisoners taken. These successes, though, were the exception and only fleeting, as the Germans counterattacked and forced the intruders back.

On the right, with the 10/Loyal North Lancs, similar scenes occurred. The barrage was responsible for many casualties, even before the objective was reached and the conditions made any attempt to get forward almost impossible, let alone fight. The toll among the officers was very high with seven dead and four wounded out of sixteen who led the men forward. By 10.00 am it was all over and those that could began to get back across the morass. The casualties among the officers of the 8/East Lancs were similarly heavy, with ten killed; it is not known how many were wounded. Their total casualties for the period in the line (14-25 November) was 18 officers and 180 other ranks.

At 11.15 am an order was issued for the relief of the 2nd Division and their replacement was to be the 32nd Division.

CHAPTER FOUR

16-19 NOVEMBER

By the morning of 16 November an easterly wind had blown away the mist and fog and the weather was clear, following overnight frost, but cold. The wind chill factor on Redan Ridge made the maximum recorded temperature of forty-one degrees seem more favourable than it really felt.

At 9.00 am General Gough convened a meeting with his corps commanders. The previous day's optimism seemed to have quickly evaporated. True, further south astride the River Ancre the 39th Division and the 63rd Division had made good progress. The 39th Division, in particular, was exceptional, capturing the remainder of the infamous Schwaben Redoubt, the village of St Pierre Divion, the Strasburg Line and advancing more than a thousand yards and taking the Hansa Line in front of Grandcourt, all in about three hours. Meanwhile, the 63rd (Royal Naval) Division had completed the capture of Beaucourt sur l'Ancre, the final assault being made with the assistance of the 13/KRRC of the 37th Division. However, the further north the conflict progressed, success was harder to find. Beaumont Hamel village was finally wrested from the Germans by the 51st (Highland) Division, but thereafter the advance ground to a halt on the slopes behind the village at the southern end of Munich and Frankfurt

Attempting to get the guns though the mud.

trenches, where the defenders resisted as stoutly (as we have seen) as their colleagues in occupation further north in the same trenches. The 51st Division had dug a new advanced position on the right of their sector and, perhaps, as a gesture of defiance after their inability to get into the real thing, called it New Munich Trench. Wagon road was the nearest the 2nd Division, whilst losing nearly 3,000 men, had got to Munich Trench, while the 3rd Division in front of Serre had made no progress at all, losing over 2,400 men in the process. The activity of these latter two divisions had used up far more men than anticipated and there were no available troops for another attempt on Serre at all. The original objectives of the 2nd Division, to drive through towards Grandcourt and Miraumont, were now assigned to the 19th Division, who would attempt to take Grandcourt from the Thiepval ridge side of the Ancre valley. The 32nd Division, now relieving the 2nd Division, were to confine their activity to capturing Frankfurt Trench which, it will be recalled, was the first objective on 13 November.

On the morning of 16 November some troops of the 32nd Division arriving at the northern end of the sector where it joined the 3rd Division near Serre could find no sign of the front line in the wilderness of the morass of mud and water filled shell holes. This should have been in the area of Wagon road. Furthermore, troops of the 3rd Division were in occupation of some of the ground, unofficially extending their sector further south, this due to the lack of any natural features in the landscape on which to get a bearing. No one was really very sure where they were.

There was little activity for the rest of the day and the next offensive was not due to take place until 18 November so as to allow plenty of time for careful planning, preparation and relief. There was, though, a lot of digging. The newly constructed southern portion of New Munich Trench was extended northwards, eventually joining up with Lager Alley. This created a new front line from which the next assault was to be made, thus shortening the distance between Wagon Road, the former position, and the first objective, Munich Trench. The distance to Munich Trench was now between 200-300 yards instead of up to 700 yards in places previously. The confusion at the northern end of the line had been resolved, too, by all this work. During the night of 16-17 November the 32nd Division took over further positions in Wagon road from the 2nd Division and then also relieved the 51st Division, who had been holding that part of the line opposite Munich Trench, where it entered their divisional sector. Thus, the 2nd Division held the line from New Munich Trench where it bordered the Beaumont-Beaucourt road to Leave Avenue in the south right up to the Quadrilateral in the north. The clear weather had enabled the Royal Flying Corps to resume its observation sorties and reports were sent back in the late afternoon of the 17 November that indicated that the Germans had abandoned their positions west of Frankfurt Trench and across the river around Grandcourt. Immediately, General Gough ordered patrols to be sent forward to occupy these positions and, in spite of protests from battalion commanders, set about issuing new orders to replace those so painstakingly prepared. Indeed, Lieutenant General Jacob informed Gough that he had information to the contrary and that the Germans were still in these positions, but to no avail and the hurried amendments to orders and eleventh hour preparations which previous experience had proved time and time again were counterproductive to success, went ahead.

At about midnight some of the patrols reported that the German trenches were a mass of shell craters and frozen mounds of earth but that the Germans were still there and working hard to improve them!

During that night it began to snow.

Saturday 18 November

The men of the 32nd Division had struggled up from Mailly Maillet on the previous day and overnight into the treacherous conditions in which they were expected to attack. Indeed, there were murmurings among some groups of men and indications that some resistance might be made to their intended fate; and who could blame them? The dreadful sights that their eyes had fallen on as the mud caked casualties

The Germans were still well dug in and determined.

Munich Trench   Frankfurt Trench

Station Trench

Station Road

To Beaumont Hamel

The Somme battlefield in the winter of 1916. Taken from a low flying aircraft, over the Ancre Valley at Beaucourt-Hamel Station.

were brought back and the terrible ordeal as narrated by those few fortunate to get back unscathed, left them in no doubt of the likely outcome of their own fate. They had arrived in a bitterly cold, wind swept and rain soaked field, just to the north east of the village, expecting to be provided with a hot meal. There was, however, no food and a cup of lukewarm tea was the only sustenance provided with which to launch themselves into the mud early the next morning. There were very few tents and the majority were expected to huddle together under their ground sheets. Pockets of dissent broke out among the men as they were roused to move forward. Officers rounded on the disaffected, drawing their revolvers and other weapons; the threat of dire and immediate retribution was sufficient to quell the revolt.

Indeed, the process of getting four battalions into position was a long and tedious one, the 17/Highland Light Infantry only consolidating their situation one hour before zero, which had been fixed for 6.10 am

Beaucourt sur l' Ancre

Beaucourt
Hamel
Station

Ancre Valley

Railway line
and road

The Division's 97 Brigade had been given the task and General Gough had insisted that all four battalions were to be used. The disposition of the troops over a frontage of just over 1,000 yards, put the 17/Highland Light Infantry on the right. Next on the right was the 16/Highland Light Infantry, and on their left was the 11/Border Regiment. On the extreme left was the 2/King's Own Yorkshire Light Infantry. Beyond the KOYLI left was the 2/Manchesters and the 15/Highland Light Infantry, who were to advance to Ten Tree Alley and secure a defensive flank.

As with so many of these assaults very little detail is known of the events as they unfolded. So many of the officers, including the adjutants, who were normally responsible for writing up the diaries, were casualties and were never able to complete their task. The diary was usually written some days later when the outcomes of a battle were then clear in broad terms and the entries reflect this and the priority it took, especially where a battalion had suffered badly.

From the outset of the attack, which commenced in darkness at 6.10 am, the Germans launched a fusillade of white flares lighting up the

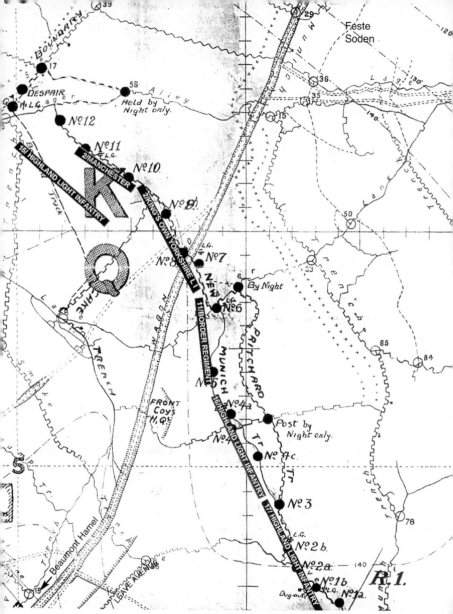

MAP 11. THE 32ND DIVISION'S DISPOSITIONS, 18 NOVEMBER.

whole area. The snow which had fallen, which had now turned to blinding sleet, provided an excellent backdrop on which the dark figures of the British soldiers were easily exposed.

We know that the left hand companies of the KOYLI, who were on the right flank of the neighbouring 14 Brigade, the 2nd Manchesters, started well and pressed forward into the snow, joining with the

74

Manchesters and reached Munich Trench in the area where the junction with Lager Alley was situated. Heavy fire was then received from a German redoubt known as *Feste Soden*, the same that had checked the initial advance of the Warwickshires on 1 July. This was in a fold in the lower ground, just behind the Lager Alley junction, which checked the advance. Meanwhile, the 15/Highland Light Infantry had experienced severe problems getting into position and were still 300 yards short of their starting point at zero hour. As a result they never really got into the fight and were isolated with no barrage to protect them. Advancing on a three company front, with a fourth fanning out behind, many were shot down even before they reached the original start line. Those that got further forward were attacked by groups of Germans who had not been cleared out by those who had gone before. To return to those men in front, the effect of the fire from the *Feste Soden* was to drive the attack to the left and, as previously in other attacks, men were travelling more or less in a northerly direction, parallel to No Man's Land. The supply of bombs was very sparse, but pressing on they went downhill crossing Ten Tree Alley moving towards Serre village, well inside the 14th Division sector. Many of the officers of both battalions were lost but the men pushed on with great determination getting into the outskirts of the village. The Germans rushed forward reinforcements which comprised the three battalions of the 169th, the first battalion of the 185th and a company

Shell fire on a snow covered landscape.

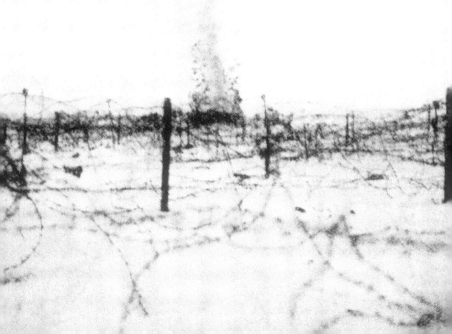

Getting the rations up through the snow.

of the 173rd, before the situation was saved. The British were isolated and most of their ammunition spent. They crouched in shell holes with little else for cover and those that could crawled back towards their own lines. The Germans mounted an attack on those still holding on from the right flank. Two companies of the III Battalion of the 66th Regiment attacked in the open from the direction of Pendant Copse and the last resistance was overcome. There were just seventy men left to surrender and a number of machine guns and other equipment was captured.

The KOYLI two right companies, though, made even less progress. They were heavily fired upon from a strong point in Munich Trench immediately they began the advance and took cover in the muddy and water filled shell holes, unable to move. At dusk they began to struggle back through the slime with their rifles useless completely clogged up with mud.

On the extreme right of the Divisional sector, in the Leave Avenue area, the two leading companies of the 17/Highland Light Infantry had the shortest distance to travel and were lying out in No Man's Land when the British barrage started to fall directly on top of them. This caused many casualties and great confusion. Urgent messages sent by Lieutenant Martin to this effect seemed to have had no correcting influence. At 7.42 am a message was received stating that the right company commander was a casualty and that the right flank was only being held by a sergeant and ten men. By 8.30 am Lieutenant MacBeth sent another message that he and Lieutenant Martin had reinforced the right flank and had set up a bombing post. Those that survived the barrage struggled forward at the appointed time towards their objective. The German troops in Munich Trench were entirely unhindered and took the opportunity to man the parapet in great strength. The barrage was intended to remain on Munich Trench for a final four minutes before ceasing to allow the attackers to get in but it was still fifty yards short for that duration As a result the 17/Highland Light Infantry were greeted by exceptionally heavy rifle and machine gunfire and were unable to make any progress. At 10.00 am, a message was received from Captain Dobson who had been forced to take cover:

Am at present in a shell hole with five unwounded men and one badly wounded man. I am slightly hit and intend waiting here till after dark when we shall endeavour to bring in Pte Bruce, badly wounded.

Frozen mud and shell holes. A scene typical of the conditions across the Redan Ridge.

He later reported:

> *I saw the Germans lining the trench in force. So near was I that I opened fire with my revolver. When the barrage was on Munich Trench the enemy's machine guns played on us all the time.*

His situation was typical of most of the rest of the survivors. Likewise, the right company of the next battalion, the 16/Highland Light Infantry, suffered similarly from the barrage and this concentration of fire and were held up, the men taking what cover they could in shell holes in the open ground. Further to the left the other companies of the 16/Highland Light Infantry fared better; the distance to Munich Trench was about 200-250 yards. This position was reached by men of the remaining companies, where heavy fighting ensued and the Scotsmen gained the upper hand, taking many prisoners. Encouraged by this success, further parties pushed on to the final objective, Frankfurt Trench, about another 200 yards distant at that point. Here further success was encountered, at least initially, and more prisoners were sent back under escort and sections of the trench captured. At this point matters deteriorated. Not enough of their fellow men on their left flank had broken through to be able to establish similar lodgements in the enemy line. The right, too, was fully exposed towards Leave Avenue, where the Germans, because of the loss of Beaumont Hamel village and further on the village of Beaucourt-sur l'Ancre, perceived that the additional loss of the Ancre heights, that is the high ground dominating the area on which both Munich and Frankfurt trenches were situated, would be a major blow they could not afford to suffer. Accordingly, they reinforced the junction of both these trenches where they met with Leave Avenue, in a strong defensive flank of two battalions of the 121st Reserve Regiment (26th Reserve Division). The concern about the 17/Highland Light Infantry right flank had been well founded.

The 11/Border Regiment also had some initial success, getting into Munich Trench and some men, joining up with the 16th Highland Light Infantry, pushed on towards Frankfurt Trench. Germans emerged and came forward with their hands up in surrender, but when near to probable capture they dropped to the ground and snipers hidden in shell holes behind them opened fire on the unsuspecting would be captors. Meanwhile, soon after daylight, Captain Ross and Second Lieutenant Greenhill along with some men of the Border Regiment and the K.O.Y.L.I. were held up by a strongpoint in Crater Lane, running from Wagon Road to Munich Trench. Sharp fighting ensued and bombing attacks were delivered. A bombing post supported by two

Sergeant Arthur Hackett
D Company, 11 (Lonsdale) Border Regiment.
Born in Workington, he was killed in action on 18 November 1916, aged 23 and is buried in Waggon Road Cemetery.
Below is Arthur's bereft fiancée, 'Auntie Forsythe' as she was known to Arthur's nephew and niece, Nelson and Hannah. She is wearing Arthur's silver cap badge on her blouse in the form of a broach. Lord Lonsdale had presented a silver cap badge to each man in the 11th Battalion.

Lewis guns, was placed in the trench and fighting went on all through the day. However, the Germans were as many as the attackers and better supplied with bombs. Coupled with that the terrible holding nature of the ground forbade the rapid forwarding of reinforcements. Some men of the Border Regiment got up to and inside the German wire and occupied shell holes, but could get no further and struggled back after dark.

By 11.00 am it was all over and the failure of the attack was conceded. During the rest of the day the stretcher parties gallantly went out and retrieved what men they could in the terrible conditions. Others made their way back to the British lines as best they could, and the remnants of 97 Brigade were gathered together in Wagon Road.

Those groups who remained out in German territory were ejected from their positions and either killed or taken prisoner. One of the escorts taking back German prisoners completely lost their way and stumbled right into the German redoubt, *Feste Soden*, where the roles were quickly reversed! There was, though, one group of men belonging mainly to the 16/Highland Light Infantry and the 11/Border Regiment, but with representatives of some of the other attacking battalions, who were still out there, established in Frankfurt Trench, who were not for giving in that easily and who would yet cause some further problems for the Germans.

This brought to a close the Battle of the Somme, at least on this part of the theatre. There was an attack in January 1917 which seemed to succeed in taking Munich Trench, but again at some cost in casualties, however there are further reports of fighting there in February too. By then both Munich and Frankfurt trenches had ceased to be recognizable and were mere depressions in the ground and the attacks passed over them without the men realising it. The real strength of Munich Trench lay beneath the ground as each spacious dugout was connected with a passage that allowed the Germans to move quickly and safely to any portion of the trench under threat.

On 20 November, following an order issued at corps headquarters that no infantrymen were to be used to assist in the awful occupation of clearing their own dead and dying from No Man's Land, about a hundred men drawn from trench mortar batteries went out under the cover of a large Red Cross flag and began the gruesome task. The Germans, probably exhausted themselves, were content to leave them unhindered and did not fire on any of these parties.

CHAPTER FIVE

FRANKFURT TRENCH

There is probably no better place to ponder on the incredible futility of the First World War, or any other war, for that matter, than to make the walk along the track to the site of Frankfurt Trench. There is absolutely nothing to see, and that is the whole point. You can then ask yourself the question, 'Why?'

Why here more than anywhere else? Well, there are certainly many other places with a similar history, but there is something different about this place, not least because we know something of the details of what occurred here. It tells you more than that. It says something about the flavour of the times, the belief in 'King and Country', of British superiority, stubbornness, self-discipline, the adjectives could continue, but most of all the reality of the 'ultimate sacrifice' and what it meant, begins to make sense, because there was no logical reason, it was completely a state of mind.

Still, we may not really understand it because it was of a different time, a different generation and our own ambitions and aspirations in the 21st century for material gain and comfort would have been as incomprehensible to them as what they did is to us today. The following extracts are taken from an account published after the war, and are written from the evidence given from survivors of the 16/ Highland Light Infantry and, therefore, contain only references to that battalion. A look through some of the archive material now available can add some more to our knowledge of what happened, but for the most part this is the story as told by the 16/Highland Light Infantry.

The defence of Frankfurt Trench is remarkable not only for its high qualities of endurance and courage, since these were not rare virtues in France and Flanders, but for the improbable nature of the whole grim and glorious exploit. If the average experienced soldier were to be asked to imagine three platoons of men to be marooned in the second line of the enemy's trenches without food or water, who would yet resist capture or total destruction for eight days in spite of savage assaults against their position, he would gravely doubt the sanity of the proposition. But this was the actual feat of arms performed. Its only military value could have been the moral effect of such resistance upon the enemy; but the accidental fact that the deed

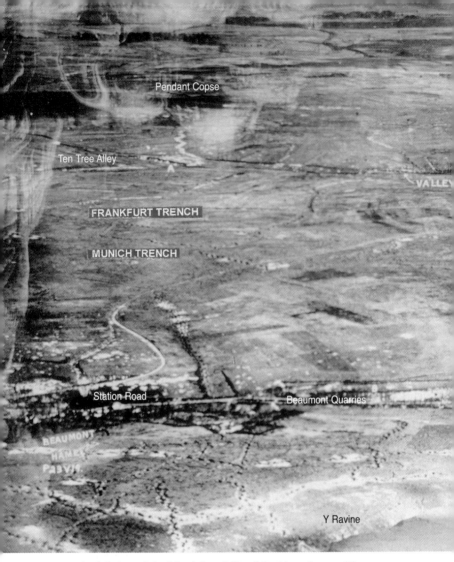

Aerial view of the Munich and Frankfurt trenches position.

served no purpose in the scheme of battle does not rob it of any of its glamour or greatness. It stands as a tremendous tribute to the character of the Scottish soldier. The German brigadier who interrogated the miserable remnant of the garrison that, as prisoners, passed into enemy hands, surveyed them in frank astonishment. "Is this what has held up the brigade for more than a week?", he asked incredulously.

The story opens on the snow swirled battlefield beyond Beaumont Hamel on the morning of 18 November 1916. D

Company and part of C Company of the 16th Highland Light Infantry have carried Munich Trench. Three platoons of D Company, leaving the rest as a mopping up party, have pushed on towards the second objective, the Frankfurt Trench.

Frankfurt Trench was not as heavily defended as Munich Trench, which was the original German third line and main objective on the opening day of the battle, 13 November. The men of the 16/Highland Light Infantry got into the trench and were in the company of a similar number of 11/Border Regiment men, even a few 2/King's Own Yorkshire Light Infantry somehow got there too. In all it is recorded that there were nine officers and about 120 men in the group that took over a stretch of the trench which contained two deep dugouts. One of these was allocated to those who were wounded The most senior officer present was Captain Welsh of the 11/Border Regiment and his fellow officers were Second Lieutenants Nixon and Brade. Of the other 11/Border men, twenty-three were wounded. Lieutenant Stewart was the most senior officer of the 16/Highland Light Infantry, and there were two other two unnamed lieutenants of the same regiment. There were also two other unnamed officers and the only other named officer was Lieutenant Rylatt of the 2/King's Own Yorkshire Light Infantry, who had been wounded. Ten of the 16/Highland Light Infantry were said to be wounded. There was one young German soldier who was wounded. Another inadvertently stumbled across the party, but he was shot dead.

To the left, several hundred yards away was a German communication trench which linked up the Munich and Frankfurt Trenches when the system was intact. Although Frankfurt Trench was flattened, with the exception of the fragment occupied by the 16/HLI, this communication trench was still serviceable to the Germans as an approach from their rear to Munich Trench, which was now manned by defenders who thus interposed themselves between the outpost and the British lines. On the right, much nearer, was another communication trench of which the Germans also retained possession. It was plainly evident to the garrison that they were holding not the nose of a salient but a strong point within the German lines. Still, the battle orders were that the objective was to be kept for 48 hours. And so consolidation proceeded.

Stock was taken of resources. There were four Lewis guns and a limited quantity of ammunition. More was got later from the bandoliers of the dead lying in the open while the garrison

Dead German machine gunner.

Smashed and deserted German trench.

handed over to the machine gunners all their SA ammunition and armed themselves with German rifles and cartridges of which there was a big cache in the dugout. Bombs were not plentiful. Of food and water there was practically none. Many of the men had already eaten iron rations and emptied their water bottles either in the scramble during the night or when, after the exertion, the trench was entered. The first pangs of hunger were appeased by iron rations taken from the dead, with no discrimination of uniform, thirst was assuaged by water skimmed from shell holes when dusk came down, and purified after a fashion by boiling over improvised lamps in which rifle oil was used as fuel and 4 by 2 cleaning flannel.

The four Lewis guns had only twenty magazines and there were only twelve bombs. These were supplemented by large quantities of German ammunition from the dugouts.

The wounded were in very bad case. Some of the flesh wounds were hideous but the only dressings were of the temporary field variety, and bandages, in some instances, were insufficient to cover the lacerated parts. Fractures had to be left alone except for the simple easing of the sufferer's position. There was no-one in the garrison with more than a working knowledge of first aid. The corporal did his utmost, it was to be a heroic service before the end came but at this moment there seemed to be no reason for despair.

The First Attack

The garrison had settled down to the state of siege on the morning of the second day. The trench was now more tenable. The collapsing walls had been revetted; machine gun emplacements had been set at vital points. Constant vigilance was required of the defenders so that every emergency could be met with the maximum strength. This day the Bosche was still without knowledge of the state of affairs or, at all events, quiescent. At night the routine search was continued for shell hole water by volunteers with water bottles packed in sandbags and slung.

The third day dawned with rising hopes of relief that were to be deferred. The sergeant of the 11 Borders had crept out in the night in an effort to break through the German cordon and bring succour. It was a mixed day. The garrison was given little time to dally with thoughts of release. The Germans had definitely

The Germans advance through the shell holes, though the dog, probably used for carrying messages, seems to be less than enthusiastic.

suspected. A strong raiding party in field grey nosed across the open and bombed the trench on the right. It was a desperate interlude. The machine guns spluttered, bombs crashed and rifles spat; trenching tools and all close quarters weapons were ready for a last stand. But the Germans repented of their rashness, this was a nest of hornets, fighting with an effectiveness beyond its numbers or condition. Leaving many casualties, the raiders faded away. The success was heartening to the garrison, but it reduced the power of further resistance, as every successive encounter must in the very nature of the case. It put the balance of strength on the side of the wounded. Therefore, it became necessary to shorten the line so as to husband the energies of the defenders. The small dugout was evacuated and the whole force concentrated on the larger one.

Company Sergeant Major S M Johnstone and Private J T Dixon of the 11/Borders left the trench at 11.30 pm and crawled into the night following a very bright star which, they had calculated, would take them in the direction of the British lines. Bright flares were being sent up from German positions in front of them (Munich Trench). They decided to make for the centre of the widest gap they could see between two flare positions. After two hours, they reached a deep trench, which was well equipped and well used, which they crossed and crawled on for some time, when they decided they were going in the wrong direction. They turned back and re-crossed the trench and continued moving on the star (which would have been leading them in a different direction by then). They seemed to have gone round in a large circle, but came to the deep trench again.They were about to cross it when a shaft of light was thrown from a dugout as someone emerged and in this light they saw a German sentry standing just a few yards away. They crawled away and managed to cross at another point but then found themselves entangled in wire. Struggling free, they crawled on, still following the star, for 'a very long time'.

A white flare went up and they saw an extended working party on their left, which they circled to the right. (It was possibly a British party as work was in progress at that time improving New Munich Trench.) This pushed them northwards, effectively away from the British lines, as they ran in a north westerly direction, but eventually they came across some forming up tapes, which they took to be British. They decided to feign injury and started to moan and groan, but this brought no response. Moving on further, they heard a voice speaking English and called out 'Is there any British Tommies there?' A voice replied 'Yes, you're all right'. A British artillery officer came forward and he directed them to Wagon Road, where they were met by men of the 16/Lancashire Fusiliers:

> Events that night conveyed the news that the Borders' sergeant had accomplished his mission. A heavy British barrage fell around the trench. The garrison waited. But there was no sound of bombs followed by that significant silence to indicate that the relief had rushed Munich Trench and was on its way. Patient hours passed with only the night noises and lights of the line. The relief had failed. It was a bad development for the garrison, although the near barrage had not caused casualties in the defence something worse was in store. The terrain had been churned up by the shells and the precious water polluted or dispersed. The bag and bottle party from the trench groped its way over the mud unavailingly after dark and returned near empty handed.

On 21 November, Major Rowan from 32nd Division headquarters travelled to the White City to examine Sergeant Johnston and Private Dixon who reported on the situation in Frankfurt Trench. It was at once proposed that he and Private Dixon should return that night, the way they had come, supported by two other men. The idea was to guide the stranded party back, the way the original journey had been made. The four men were to be supported by strong patrols, who would fend off any attempt by the Germans to counterattack. The two men could not have relished the thought of this and little is known of their progress, except that it is recorded that they returned at 8.45 am the next morning and reported that the attempt had failed, not surprisingly.

Meanwhile, colleagues of the battalions trapped in Frankfurt Trench also made two attempts to get through. Captain Hunter of the 11/Borders led a strong party forward to try and make contact with Captain Welsh. This failed and they returned at 4.30 am. A joint party of 16/Highland Light Infantry and 11/Borders also returned unsuccessful.

Fresh courage was inspired in the wan and weary trench on the fourth morning by the sight of an observation plane with the familiar British markings skimming low over No Man's Land obviously in search of their whereabouts. Moving discreetly, for now they were under close surveillance, the garrison tried to attract the attention of the pilot. A signaller, using pieces of torn shirt, crawled out and lay on his back in a hollow to make flag signals. The plane, to the delight of all in the trench crowded to watch, zoomed down to the reconnoitre and sped away back to the British lines. After an interval it came back with five others, a heartening sight for isolated men. Torch signals were flashed from the planes urging the garrison to hold out as relief was coming. This was distinctly more cheerful, and it was almost as good as salvation itself when the planes returned next day with more reassuring signals.

Four days have reduced the garrison to a pitiful plight. Hunger was the least of their tortures, at least, the lack of food caused no great inconvenience after the first effects of fasting were over, except when physical effort was required and the feeling of symptoms of starvation became apparent. The thirst was more intolerable. The wounded were laid out on the floor of a small gallery beyond the pillars that ran lengthwise along the dugout and partitioned it into two long corridors. Candles had long since guttered out and it was dark as the pit of Tophet down there. The wounded were not visible and men were silently dying without the others knowing their tragedies. Many of the wounds were gangrenous; there was no water to wash bandages, no antiseptics to stay the creeping death, no anodynes to ease the burning pains, no soporifics. The main corridor, nearest the two stairways which ran parallel to the gallery of the wounded,

Ready and waiting.

*served as quarters for the active garrison. Sleep was almost out
of the question owing to the disturbance caused by the hourly
reliefs stumbling to their places. The stairway, too, was
crammed. Some of the men preferred the cold and the exposure
of the open trench, their only blanket the wall of the parapet. The
moral and physical effort of these conditions was to make the
organisation of the defence and the maintaining of its efficiency
more and more, as time went on, a superhuman task.*

Two Great Soldiers

*It is almost a law of nature that every great crisis produces
men big enough to meet it. The man of the moment in this stretch
was a citizen soldier, a sergeant who, by right of seniority,
assumed the duties of sergeant major. He was a married man
and before the war he rose to foreman with the Glasgow
Corporation. A natural leader strong in character, but with that
robust cheerfulness which is comfort and strength in dangerous
places, he was the heart and soul of the defence during this
critical period. He never seemed to rest, he was always
everywhere setting a great example of cool fortitude, out with the
reconnaissance and water parties, down in the awful dugout
fathering his men, full of nerve and courage in the hottest part of*

the defence. During the night and especially in that stomachless hour before dawn, he went about breezy and imperturbable with a song on his lips.

There was another who outstandingly, with his sergeant major, shared the unconquerable spirit. He was the lance jack in charge of machine guns. This NCO was the son of a sergeant of the Scots Greys and had been born in Ireland. The soldierly qualities inherited from his parent were self evident in the verve with which he fought his guns, upon the steady calculation of this man the successful chances of resistance first depended and he never swerved a fraction from his trust.

The enduring heroism of these two non commissioned officers helped wonderfully to keep stern and steady the will of the garrison to resist to the end. To this high purpose they ultimately sacrificed their lives. The sergeant major's last ringing words were "no surrender boys". Both were recommended for the Victoria Cross, and they were both posthumously mentioned in dispatches.

The Aeroplane Message

The fifth day dawned. Still the trench was in the hands of the defenders. The relief attack promised in the message from the aeroplanes was launched from the British lines, but it never came through Munich Trench. The barrage again was fierce and the garrison was driven underground, the dugout entrances being blown in. When quiet had been restored the soul sick garrison crept back into the trench and the endless watch. Later in the day a British aeroplane came over and dropped a message in a bag. The arctic wind tore up the bag as it fell, it opened and the paper was driven away in a swirl to the German trenches. Observing what had happened, the pilot signalled by flasher. This signal was read differently. Some of the garrison interpreted it as "coming tomorrow", others read it as "come in tomorrow". Only a slight literal variation but what a world of difference. The plane had gone and left a legacy of confusion. The garrison was in a quandary. There was a thoughtful conference, the council of waiting prevailed. This was a big decision for all knew that the barrages had left water in only pitifully and poisonous trickles.

At 1.00 pm on 22 November another two men returned from the stranded party. This time a lance corporal and a private (unnamed) succeeded in making the hazardous journey to corroborate what Johnston and Dixon had said. They reported that an attempt to break out would be made that night by the stranded party. A mixed group of 16/Highland Light Infantry and 11/Borders under the command of one officer went forward and lay out in No Man's Land in front of Munich Trench but they heard and saw nothing. Meanwhile, that day a conference had been held at Divisional headquarters in Mailly Maillet at which General Gough was present.

An attack to rescue the stranded men was planned and was originally intended to be a full 96 Brigade assault. However, it was found that when orders were being prepared it was apparent that all battalions were well under strength and the men exhausted. So it was left to the 16/Lancashire Fusiliers, supported by a party of the 2/Inniskillings, to attempt the breakthrough and rescue. In preparation for the attack the artillery was ordered to put down a heavy barrage on Munich Trench to cut the wire, which was reported to be intact.

The attack was under the command of Captain C W Merryweather, 16/Lancashire Fusiliers, and consisted of three companies of the Fusiliers, numbering 240 men and one company of eighty Inniskllings. It was delivered in daylight, (one diary reports this as being 10.00 am, while another states 3.30 pm) in the area between Walker Avenue and Crater Lane. The Inniskillings were on the extreme right of the attack, resting on Walker Avenue. The plan was for waves one, three, and four to attack Munich Trench while the second wave would be held up but

The troops struggle forward to their positions

then pass through and advance on Frankfurt Trench. The first waves went forward and got into Munich Trench, the second wave came through and pushed on but ran into the British barrage. Captain Merryweather was seen to fall on the parapet of Munich Trench, urging his men forward. Lieutenant Higginson reorganised the men that were left and pushed on again towards Frankfurt Trench, but was not seen again. A report said he was hit by enfilade fire from the right. Second Lieutenant Rylands was sent forward after Higginson was seen to fall, but he too was wounded. It is difficult to know exactly what happened, survivors said that exceptionally heavy fire came from the communication trench on the right known as Walker Avenue. With Crater Lane on the left also in German hands

Lieutenant H B Rylands 16/Lancashire Fusiliers, killed in the attack to relieve Frankfurt Trench. Commemorated on the Thiepval Memorial to the Missing.

a more suicidal attempt can not be imagined, with frontal fire and enfilade from both flanks to contend with. Fighting continued in Munich Trench until all the stragglers from the second wave had returned and the attack was then called off. The only time given for this was 4.30 pm, which makes the more likely time for the start of the attack as 10.00 am. Lieutenant Rylands was missing and attempts to bring in the wounded were led by the chaplain, Reverend W H Fawkes, who dragged several men back to safety from in front of the wire protecting Munich Trench. The Fusiliers lost seven officers and 224 other ranks. The commanding officer sent the following report to brigade headquarters.

Lieutenant F C Caird. Served with the Royal Naval Division at Antwerp and Gallipoli before being commisioned in the Inniskilling Fusiliers. Wounded just prior to the attempt to relieve Frankfurt Trench, was taken back, but died and is buried in Puchevillers Military Cemetery.

With further reference to the attack on November 23rd, I have examined all the men who came back and can find only one who got any considerable distance past Munich Trench. This is an intelligent man, one of the battalion snipers, and he was on the left of the wave during the advance. He got up to the barrage 150 yards beyond Munich Trench but states that he could see

92

nobody else with him and he retired when the barrage lifted as there was no one to go forward with him. He states that there was some machine gun fire mostly from his left while he was advancing and that this became very heavy when he turned to go back and on his way back he saw no sign of anyone in Frankfurt Trench, the line of which he could see quite clearly.

Other reports say that there were about 15 men beyond Munich Trench with Lieutenant Higginson but these were on the right of the sniper mentioned above. I think that the failure of the advance to reach Frankfurt Trench was owing to:

1. Machine Gun fire from the flanks. 2. The fact that some of the advanced men ran into the barrage 3. The fact that the officers and all the NCO's became casualties.

C M Abercrombie Lt. Col. C.O. 16 Lancashire Fusiliers.

Little is known of the Inniskillings except that Captain S E Clarke was in command and that four officers were casualties, including Second Lieutenants C F Beverland and J Mc N McKinstry who were killed.

MAP 12. THE ATTEMPTED RELIEF OF THE PARTY CUT OFF IN FRANKFURT TRENCH. NOTE THREE DUGOUTS ARE MARKED ON THE ORIGINAL MAP. (Walker Avenue was previously known as New Trench.)

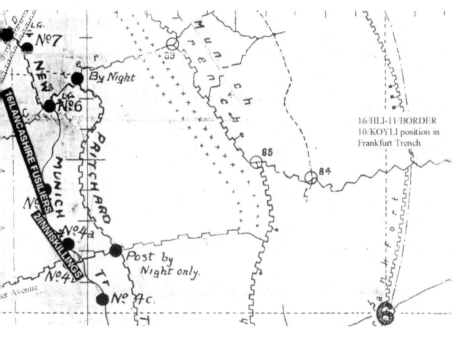

The Germans, probably encouraged by the translation of the strayed message of the previous day or else perhaps just impatient of this obstinate foreign body in their trench system, launched a powerful attack from front and flanks on the afternoon of the sixth day, 23 November. It almost succeeded in reducing the stronghold. The shelling and the sentries' warning aroused the defenders, but it was difficult for exhausted men to dash up dugout steps. The slow painful response to the call allowed the Germans to get so close that one of the dugout entrances was bombed before serious resistance was offered. But when the full strength of the defence was mustered a primitive struggle developed at close quarters. All the odds were on the attackers, they were slept and fed and well armed. But the men with no food in their stomachs put to rout all the Napoleonic maxims and uncompromisingly routed the Germans who left eight prisoners in the hands of the garrison. The heaviest blow to the defence was the loss of the lance corporal of the machine guns, he who had been the Horatius of the trench. A sniper's bullet took him when the fight was over and he stood in his gun emplacement. [He was Lance Corporal John Veitch, 16/Highland Light Infantry.]

Against the purple sky of the seventh dawn in Frankfurt Trench the sentries were awed by a foreboding spectacle. Fresh German troops were entering the sector, their bucket shaped steel helmets in a long procession bobbed up and down in a black silhouette in the communication trench against the paling sky. This day the new German commander sent a message under cover of a white flag, and in custody of an Inniskilling Fusilier who had been captured in one of the unsuccessful attempts to relieve the besieged trench. The purport of this document was that if the garrison threw in their hand the German commander assured them of good treatment. If they didn't, he added menacingly, then he would come over in staggering force and they could take what was coming to them.

The message was pondered with the gravity it deserved. Who could have blamed that starving, famished and frozen post if in a moment of irresolution its garrison had gladly taken the only escape that now appeared to remain from death by violence or more lingeringly in some other way? Perhaps the Bosche threat, from his point of view, was poor diplomacy; at events the temper of the garrison was stiffened and both threat and offer were

PRIVATE MATTHEW HAWKESWORTH was born in East Stamford, Lincolnshire, 12 July 1882, where his father was recorded as being a blacksmith. The family moved to Nottinghamshire to take advantage of the higher wages being paid in the mining industry at that period. In the census of 1901 he was living with his parents in the mining town of Hucknall. He was a bricklayer who practised his trade in the local collieries. He married Ada Hudson in 1904 and had four children. Despite the fact that his children were young (the youngest was four years old when he died), he must have volunteered early in the war, although at his age he had no need to do so. It is likely that he thought, as did so many others, that the war would not last long. He served in France in the Notts and Derby Regiment and was transferred to the 16th Lancashire Fusiliers following the decimation of that battalion during the early battles of the Somme. His widow never remarried and only visited his grave on one occasion (in 1921) with the assistance of a grateful government who issued her a passport for a 'once only' journey. She had three sisters and two brothers, both brothers having been seriously wounded in 1915. For the rest of their lives they were never fit enough to work again.

Private Hawkesworth, aged 34, was killed in the attempted relief of Frankfurt Trench and is buried in Waggon Road Cemetery, where relatives still visit his grave.

ignored as well as the possibilities to which silence consigned a lot. After a polite interval the Germans indicated that they meant business by shelling heavily. This strafe did more damage than the annoyed Germans could have hoped. The sergeant major, fearing that the attack was about to begin, sprang to the parapet and was struck and killed by a fragment of shell as he watched. He died shouting defiance. Yet the fighting spirit of the handful of troops rose above this tragedy. [This was Sergeant George A Lee, 16/Highland Light Infantry.]

There was no water found that night. This was the beginning of the end. All through the darkness and the biting cold the

---

SERGEANT J E PRESTON was among the company of 2nd Inniskillings who attempted to rescue the men trapped in Frankfurt Trench. He never returned. On enquiry from relatives or others, the army usually made detailed attempts to discover the fate of a soldier killed in action. This included interviewing men who survived and taking evidence from any other source. Sometimes they would put relatives in touch with such witnesses. Relatives often advertised in local papers for information and this sometimes produced results. Sergeant Preston's family tried to find out more about his death and did find some witnesses. He was, though, never to have an identified grave and is commemorated on the Thiepval Memorial to the Missing of the Somme. His grandson, Norman Gray, still visits the place where the attack took place and feels that his grandfather may be one of two unidentified Inniskilling graves in Waggon Road Cemetery, as there is evidence he was actually buried. There are fifteen names on the Thiepval Memorial in all and with three unknown graves. This leaves twelve men totally unaccounted for. Perhaps they lay somewhere deep in the mud where even today's big ploughs cannot disturb them.

27/7084/2.
(If replying, please
quote above No.)

ARMY FORM B. 104—82A.

_____ Record Office,

_____

_____ 191

Madam,

It is my painful duty to inform you that no further news having
been received relative to (No.) *7084* (Rank) *Sergeant*
(Name) *John Pruston*
(Regiment) *RNIS. FUS.*
who has been missing since *23rd Nov. 1916*, the Army Council
have been regretfully constrained to conclude that he is dead, and that
his death took place on the *23rd Nov. 1916.* (or since).

By His Majesty's command I am to forward the enclosed
message of sympathy from Their Gracious Majesties the King and Queen.
I am at the same time to express the regret of the Army Council at the
soldier's death in his Country's service.

I am,

Madam,

Your obedient Servant.

Margaret Pruston

...............................Capt.
for ... Infantry Records, Dublin.

Officer in charge of Records.

Wt. 6167/M 2824. 30M. 8/17. R. & L., Ltd. Forms/B/104—82A.   P.T.O.

BRITISH RED CROSS SOCIETY,

51 Dawson Street,

DULIN.

Telephone: DUBLIN 4590

1st October 1917.

Mrs Preston,
    Suffolk,
        Dunmurry,
            Belfast.

Re Sergt. J. Preston 7084
2nd Royal Innisk.Fusiliers A.Coy.
K. Nov.23/11/16.

Dear Madam,

We send you two reports from men of his Battalion, both of which substantially agree. We should hope that his Grave is registered by this time.

L/Cpl. J. Marsland 18804, 2nd R.Inniskilling Fus.A.Coy. Ebrington Barracks Hospital, Londonderry, home address, 12 a, Netherfield Road, South Averton,Liverpool, states:-

"I identified Sergt. Preston's body. I am certain it was "he, I could recognise him. It was moonlight,9.30.p.m. when "the Bodies were found. L/Cpl.Preston Was Sergt."

L/Cpl. Campbell 10588, 2nd R.Innisk.Fusilier, A.Coy. Ebrington Barracks Hospital,Londonderry, home address, 27 Carrington Street, Belfast, states:-

"On November 23 1916 at Beaumont Hamel L/Cpl.Preston "was killed (he was L/Sergt.) This I know by hearsay but later "I was with a working party and found several bodies and "among them was Sergt.Preston's, he could be identified. "Pte.Arbuckle 2nd R.Innis.Fus.A.Coy. also identified Sgt. "Preston's body. There was shell fire and the bodies just then "were not touched, later on a party came up to bury them,but "I was not one of the burying party. When I saw them they "were just lifted and I had not time to examine where Serg.t "Preston had been hit.He was buried at BeaumontHamel.

volunteers with their bags and bottles searched the shell holes even to the rim of the Munich Trench from where they could hear the Germans speaking. There, almost discovered, one of the men struck a pool of precious water. Several bottles were hurriedly filled and the post successfully regained with the trophy. When the fluid was poured out it stank villainously and was highly discoloured. The corporal in charge of the wounded declined to give it to his casualties in spite of their cravings. Those who drank contracted a virulent form of typhoid.

BRITISH RED CROSS SOCIETY,
(CO. DUBLIN BRANCH).
AND
ST. JOHN AMBULANCE ASSOCIATION.

ENQUIRY DEPARTMENT

51 DAWSON STREET,
DUBLIN.
2nd November 1917

Mrs Preston,
   Scarva St.,
     Banbridge Co.Down

     Re Sgt. J. Preston 7084
   2nd R.Innisk.Fusiliers, A. Coy.
     M. Nov.23/16.

Dear Madam,

     Since writing you yesterday we have received the following more definite report and greatly regret its nature, coming from a responsible N.C.O. You are at liberty of course to write Sergt. Donaldson at Derry. If you do perhaps you would tell us what he has to say.about his burial.

     Sgt. Donaldson 10421, 2nd R.Innis. Fus.C.Coy. Ebrington Barracks, Hutt Londonderry, home address, 23 Outram St.Belfast, states:-

     "On Nov.23/16 at Beaumont Hamel at 7 p.m. when coming in to their own lines again he passed Sergt.Preston (he was Sgt. not L/Cpl.) at 2 or 3 yds distance from him, lying on the ground in No Man's Land, dead he was sure, but could not say where he had been wounded. There was not time to stop, it had been a bombing raid in an attack, all the men said as they passed "That was Sgt. Preston lying there".Informant says he knows Sgt. Preston was a time serving soldier. He was about 5'6", dark moustache, slight."

     Yours faithfully,

     Edmund A. Trouton

     Hon.Sec.to the Dpt.

The promised German attack came on the eighth day at what hour no-one can remember for time was now eternity. It was in force and from every point of the compass. Sentries and gunners were shot down or stricken with bombs before all of the effectives in their listless state could emerge from cover. The Germans promptly bombed the dugout. If they knew, they stopped not to consider the reeking hospital below. The shouts of the eight German prisoners held as hostages arrested the process of sheer annihilation, otherwise no-one would have lived to tell the tale.

The Trench Falls

The incomparable stand was over. Fifteen of the hundred were left unwounded but so woefully weak from the effects of thirst, want and incipient disease that they could scarcely keep their feet and staggered dizzily. They were ordered to carry back the wounded to the German lines. None of those who recount their experiences are aware how they bore the weight of the stretchers. As they carried their burdens in relays, British shells were falling, one of which killed a member of the German escort. Every one of the prisoners expected to be slaughtered outright. Perhaps it was an unjust thought, but the ranks of machine guns mounted in the open lent colour to the fear although, in clearer moments, the prisoners might have accepted the presence of this armament as a great tribute. The Germans endured the casualty without a murmur. Afterwards there was a stupid investigation in the Brigadier's dugout and then a nightmare march of twelve miles over mud and ruin until the little party was lodged in the cellars of a French chateau. The prison camps and hospitals, with their extraordinary life followed. Two of the men who were taken prisoner died in captivity; one was shot by the Germans for the unwarlike offence of accepting a piece of bread from a French inhabitant.

CHAPTER SIX

VISITING THE BATTLEFIELDS

The maps contained within this book will enable the visitor to find the way around the area on which the narrative is based. However, especially if visits to other parts of the battlefields are intended, and a route to the Somme area is required there are good maps available. The yellow Michelin 1/200, 000 (1cm:2km) series give good detail and will guide you on your journey south from Calais and around the area. The numbers required are 51 and 52. The Commonwealth War Graves Commission has produced a booklet with all the relevent Michelin maps overprinted with most of the war cemeteries, and with a useful index. Sometimes, though, it is difficult to read the map as there are so many of them. There is also the larger Serie Bleue IGN maps (1cm-250m). The map covering this book is 2407 O, Acheux-en-Amienois. To cover the majority of the battlefields you will need another three maps, 2407 E, 2408 O and 2408 E. These maps can be purchased at Maison de la Presse in Albert, which is on the left of the square as you stand on the steps at the west end of the Basilique. It will be cheaper to buy them in France than in the United Kingdom, or elsewhere, beforehand.

The quickest route to the Somme from the United Kingdom is to cross from Dover to Calais (or Folkestone to Calais via the Shuttle). There is also a more economical crossing by ferry from Dover to Dunkirk. From Calais follow the signs for the A26 to Arras and Paris. The autoroute will be quiet. Continue to the junction of the A26/A1, continuing to follow the signs to Paris. As you join the A1 the traffic will be heavier but the journey is only a short one to Exit 16 for Bapaume. The distance from Calais is about ninety miles. From Bapaume take the D929 to Albert.

You should book your accommodation in advance. Although the growth in numbers of those visiting the battlefields has been reflected in an increase in available accommodation, an imbalance still exists. Remember the area is rural and agricultural, the nearest large hotels are in Amiens or Arras.

If you have nowhere to stay, call at the Office du Tourisme in Albert. This is opposite the Basilique, towards the right. I have included a selective list of accommodation as an appendix to this section to assist the reader in making an advance booking.

What you need to have in your luggage will depend on what time of year you decide to visit. Winter can be colder on the Somme and wetter too! Full waterproofs, together with wellingtons or good boots are essential. Warm clothing should include gloves and headwear. A day sack is also useful to put in your camera, compass, small first aid kit, penknife, bottle opener, corkscrew and refreshments, books, maps, pens and other bits and pieces. Summer can still present wet conditions, even though the average rainfall is less than in Britain. It can also be considerably hotter in summer, and temperatures can soar above thirty degrees centigrade. Protection in the form of headwear and sun cream is essential. Always have available plenty to drink, not necessarily alcohol, for that can be counterproductive in more ways than one.

Driving in the Somme area should present few problems. The roads, with a few exceptions, are much quieter and in this area you are as likely to meet a British registered car as a French one. There are some important differences to remember and the first and most important one, if you are British, is to remember to drive on the right. Of course friends from the U.S.A. and some other countries will not be too concerned about this. The most dangerous time is when first setting out after a halt. It is very easy to pull out on to the left of the carriageway with potentially disastrous results.

The cheapness and availability of alcohol, together with the distance from home, should not lure the visitor into believing it is all right to drink and drive. The alcohol limit (50 milligrams) is lower than at home in Britain and it is rigorously enforced by regular road blocks for mass on-the-spot testing and there is no escape!

It is also a legal requirement to carry a warning triangle and a set of replacement light bulbs. All documents should be carried too; this includes: insurance, driving licence and registration document. Your insurance should include full European Cover, obtainable through your insurance company. Failure to do this could result in your being insured for only third party under current EC law. Breakdown insurance is a matter for your own judgement. There are several garages in Albert who act as agents for most popular makes of cars and I know several instances of their services being well received.

The final point on motoring is to beware of the rule 'Priority from the Right'. In all cases, unless marked otherwise, you must give way to the traffic approaching anywhere from the right. This includes traffic approaching you ostensibly from ahead but offset to the right. In the country, the sign to look for is a cross (X) which normally indicates

Snow covered headstones in the Ancre British Cemetery.

priority from the right at the next junction. If you have priority the junction will normally be marked with broken lines, as at home, or there will be a road sign with a pointed arrow with a bar through it. In urban areas, unless marked otherwise, all junctions are priority from the right.

As a member of the EC, the UK has a reciprocal arrangement with France and other European member countries for obtaining medical treatment. By obtaining forms E111 from any Post Office you will be able to take advantage of this, but in the case of France this falls well short of what you can expect at home. In the first place, you may be asked for money 'up front'. Treatment and any drugs must be paid for and then claimed back in the same way that a French national is required to do from the local social security office. Only a proportion of the costs will be refunded – between 60% and 80%. Medical treatment can be expensive and the claimant could still be presented with a substantial bill. It should also be remembered that such things as re-arranged hotel and travel expenses or repatriation are not covered. No special inoculations are necessary but it is advisable to have tetanus injections. The Somme is a high risk area, because of its history, all agricultural workers are obliged to have injections. There are many agencies offering travel insurance – a few pounds for a few days would seem a reasonable investment. There are also now annual policies and they are good value for money which offer an unlimited number of trips.

Always have your passport with you. The French have a national identity card and the Gendarmes and Police could ask you to provide proof of identity. The Somme region is a quiet and, on the whole, a trouble free area but crime does exist. Be careful not to leave valuables in your car. There have been instances of visitors' cars being broken into while the owners were away walking or visiting a distant cemetery.

Albert is the largest centre of population, most of the soldiers involved in the fighting on the Somme would be familiar with it. It was a garrison town just behind the British lines and was regularly shelled by German artillery. Its most famous landmark is the Madonna and Child on top of the Basilque which hung precariously for most of the duration of the war. It was said at the time that when it fell the war would end. Many years later, a veteran friend of mine, Alan Walmsley of the Duke of Wellington's Regiment, was always sceptical about the legend of the Golden Virgin. With his dry northern sense of humour he said 'That couldn't be right, you know, 'cos the bloody Royal Engineers wired it up!' Today it stands above the town and shines out at night, a beacon which can be seen from many points across the surrounding countryside. The floodlighting was renewed in 1996 as part of the commemoration of the 80th Anniversary of the Battle of the Somme. In 2000, a fuller renovation of the building was commenced and it is now pristine and gleaming in its gold paint. It is in Albert where most visitors do their shopping and buy fuel. The underground museum dedicated to the First World War is housed in tunnels used as shelters during the Second World War and the entrance is signposted near the west end of the Basilique. A very substantial museum is situated in Peronne, about sixteen miles to the east of Albert, and is a good wet weather day alternative.

Finally, the visitor to the Somme will almost certainly come across the debris of war. Although recently there have been renewed efforts to clear up live shells, hand grenades and mortar bombs as they come to light, there are still many of these potentially lethal objects about. It is as well to remember that the cemeteries we visit and memorials we look at represent tens of thousands killed by these explosives and the increase in 'accidents' in recent years have caused the authorities to take certain steps to reduce the risk of injury or death. It is now forbidden to possess anything – even a simple .303 cartridge – that is live. It is also forbidden to possess anything that has been defused and

A padre tends graves in Carnoy Military Cemetery. Note the soldiers in the trenches on the bank behind.

The cemetery today

to possess a metal detector. If you do come across any human remains, the first action should be to report it to the local Gendarmes. The Commonwealth War Graves Commission at Beaurains, near Arras, will not normally attend unless called by the Gendarmes, but assistance could be sought from the local teams of the Commission's workers who will be seen frequently about the area. The nearest workbase is at the Thiepval Memorial and there is also one at the hamlet of Serre.

WHERE TO STAY
Listed Hotels in Albert

***   Royal Picardie, Route d'Amiens 80300
Tel (0033) 322753700
Fax (0033) 322756019

**   La Basilique, 3 Rue Gambetta 80300
Tel (0033) 322750471
Fax (0033) 322751047

*   Hotel de la Paix, 39 Rue Victor Hugo 80300
Tel (0033) 322750164
Fax (0033) 322754417

Listed Chambres d'Hôtes (Bed & Breakfast)
These three are very local and within walking distance of the area covered in the book.

+   Nr Beaumont Hamel
Les Galets, Route de Beaumont,
Tel (0033) 322762879
Auchonvillers 80560
Fax (0033) 322762879

Grandcourt, 9 Rue de Beaucourt 80300
Tel (0033) 322748158
Fax (0033) 322748165

+   Auchonvillers
Avril Williams Guesthouse,
Tel(0033) 322762366
10 Rue Delattre, 80560 (meals for non residents available)

+   These are British owned establishments.

Other Recommended Establishments
There are few facilities in the battlefield area itself for the tourist.

However those looking for refreshment or somewhere to have a meal will find the following satisfactory:

Authuille
Auberge de la Valleé d'Ancre
A good quality restaurant at reasonable prices
6 Rue Moulin, 80300   Tel 0322751518

Ovillers
Le Poppy
A cheap but good 'Les Routiers' style restaurant
4 Route Bapaume, 80300   Tel 0322754545

Pozieres
Le Tommy Bar, cafeteria and trench museum
Rue Albert   Tel 0322748284

Ulster Memorial Tower
Thiepval
Light refreshments and toilets

Newfoundland Memorial
Beaumont Hamel
Toilets available.

Delville Wood
South African Memorial and Museum
Light refreshments and toilets

CHAPTER SEVEN

THE SOMME BATTLEFIELDS

The Somme river flows through the chalk uplands of the département to which it gives his name on its journey to the Bay of the Somme on the coast and thence into the sea at St Valery. To flow is probably the most accurate description to use when describing the Somme river. While there is a man-made canal that still offers a profitable trade to barge owners, the river itself consists of a series of lakes or lagoons, some created with the assistance of man. They spread over a wide area of the bottom of the valley, around which are clustered little chalets and huts or caravans in the ownership of the many fishermen the water attracts. The water levels are all controlled by a network of sluices. The area is rich in wildlife, many fish, of course, but also numerous birds and water fowl and I have seen red squirrels and otters. On its way the river passes through the pleasant towns of Peronne and Corbie, the latter with its fine abbey, and on to Amiens. This is the 'county town' or capital of the departement and among some other impressive buildings there is large cathedral, the nave of which is the highest in Europe. At its apex it is the equivalent of a block of flats with thirteen storeys.

The countryside around the area is entirely rural with open and rolling fields commanding long distance views, interspersed with little wooded valleys accommodating small streams and rivers. It is perfect walking, fishing and hunting country. Its soil has long been productive and suitable for sugar beet, potatoes, maize and grain crops, although recent European agricultural policy has seen a marked decline in dairy herds and cattle.

Over the centuries war has never been far from the Somme. As far as the British are concerned, apart from the battle in 1916, the most notable must be the Battle of Crécy.

Crécy is small town, situated on the river Maye in the west of the département. It was here on 26 August 1346 that England's martial glory achieved its greatest height during the 'Age of Chivalry' when Edward III gained an overwhelming victory over Phillip VI of France and his allies.

It is interesting to recount some of the detail of this conflict and compare it with what happened nearly six hundred years later. Then, the English and Welsh were the perceived invaders, and initially numbered about 15,000 when they landed in Normandy. Making their way south burning and looting, they arrived at the Somme about 10,000 strong. An account written at the time survives today.

It was the evening of Friday 25 August, and the king was encamped on the bank of the Somme, when, over the river bank which the English had already crossed, came Phillip, the French tyrant, and with him the kings of Bohemia and Majorca, with a vast army composed of eight great divisions.

The French shouted exultantly at the king of England and his men, and on both sides of the river soldiers waded into the shallows or stood on the banks and shook spears like jousters at a tournament. The king of England sent messages to the king of France offering him a safe passage across the river by the ford and proposing that he select a place fit for a battle. But that coward Phillip de Valois, though he had previously threatened to pursue the king of England, was now unwilling to engage in battle and turned aside, as if to cross the river at some other point. All night, Edward III waited for him. The following day, a Sunday, King Edward moved his army to the field of Crécy, where they came upon the king of France.

The French amassed 40,000 to repel the enemy. On 1 July 1916, the

A peaceful scene in the Ancre valley. The Ulster Memorial Tower stands on the horizon.

Germans were similarly outnumbered by about four to one. The weather, also, was very wet before the battle and this was to have a marked outcome effect on the outcome of the battle.

Leading one division of the French were 6,000 Genoese cross bowmen, and it was expected that this newer weapon would easily put paid to the English archers who were still using the older long-bow. In 1916 it was the Germans who had put their trust in the modern machine-gun, but the outcome was to be entirely different. Prior to the battle the English and Welsh archers put their bow strings under their helmets to keep them dry. It seems that the crossbowmen failed to take this precaution and their bolts failed to reach King Edward's army, who

Edward III crossing the Somme before the Battle of Crécy.

Charge of the French cavalry on the English bowmen at the Battle of Crécy.

were ranged on the upper slopes of the hill. A natural hedge grew across their front and the men had dug trenches beyond this a foot wide and similar in depth. King Edward deployed his three divisions with the bowmen on each flank. The right flank was commanded by his son, the Black Prince and the left flank division by the earls of Northampton and Hereford. The battle commenced at 3 o'clock in the afternoon. The English were much quicker in firing their arrows, which, according to an eye witness, 'fell like snow' right on target, while they were unhindered by the reply. Being on the defensive, and static, suited the smaller English army, as it did for the Germans in 1916. Indeed, the size of the French forces proved to be its ultimate undoing, as it was unduly cramped for space on the battle front. Seeing that the enemy were not inconvenienced, King Phillip sent in his cavalry and they could not get through without riding over their own comrades, causing chaos and many casualties.

Loud screams arose from the French crossbow men trampled by the great horses and from the knight's chargers who had been wounded with arrows, while the French ranks were thrown into further confusion by the stumbling of the horses. Many fell as they fought with the English, wounded by axes, lancers and sword, while many who had suffered no honourable war wound were simply crushed to death in the midst of their own numerous army.

Old trench lines on the north bank of the Ancre.

In the heart of this ferocious battle, the noble spirited Edward of Woodstock, King Edward III's eldest son, who at that time was sixteen years old, was showing the French his admirable bravery at the head of his division. He stabbed horses, killed knights, struck helmets, snapped lances or sword, craftily parried blows, aided his men, defended himself, helped up fallen comrades, and encouraged all to good deeds by his own example. Nor did he cease from his noble efforts until the enemy retired behind the mound of their own dead.

As the unsuspecting British were to do in 1916, the French went forward uphill into carefully prepared positions enfiladed with strong flanking fire. They had ridden in great numbers into 'the valley of death, so called, as the English and Welsh archers shot down the horsemen. Those that survived then stumbled into the pits that had been dug and many horses were brought down. King Edward, commanding the centre division, then sent in his men which included many knights, who had been ordered to dismount, leaving their horses behind. The furious hand to hand fighting continued until after dark, with the Earls of Northampton and Hereford and the Black Prince, the Prince of Wales, leading the attack, seeking out their opposite numbers. No comfortable rear headquarters here, then! However, King Edward did watch from a windmill on a hill in the rear.

Fifteen times the French attacked but could make no impression on

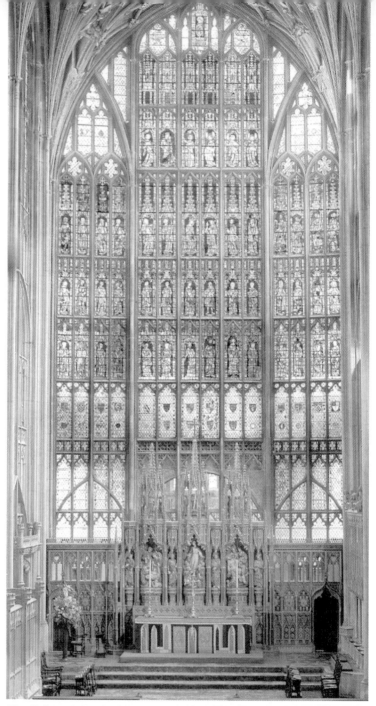

The Crécy window in Gloucester Cathedral.

the narrow battle front. At last, under cover of darkness, King Phillip was dragged reluctantly away by his remaining attendants, leaving dead on the field his allies King John of Bohemia and James, King of Majorca, together with no fewer than eleven great princes from the three kingdoms also slain that day. About 4,000 of his knights were killed and more than 30,000 of his men. Eighty French standards were captured. The English losses were very small. The next day the battle entered its last phase when, with great determination, the French attacked for the sixteenth and last time. In four battle lines they advanced on their enemy and a long and fierce battle ensued. At last the French retreated and King Edward's men, who had previously maintained full discipline and resisted taking any rich prisoners, broke ranks and pursued the French in a bloodthirsty charge.

It was reported that the Black Prince took from the battlefield the shield and helmet belonging to King John on which were emblazoned, three ostrich feathers and the motto *Ich Dien* (I Serve), and adopted them as his own, and this is how they became associated with Wales. This story, though, is doubted by some authorities.

Crécy, is a short journey along the pretty Authie valley from the 1916 battlefields and can be combined with a trip to the coast and the Bay of the Somme. There is a viewing platform and an orientation table, sited probably near to where King Edward watched the battle and made his famous response to his sixteen year old son's call for reinforcements. 'Let the boy win his spurs.' It is not difficult to imagine the scenes of dreadful suffering and death, that were enacted on that day.

The Black Prince seemed to spend more time in France than in Britain, but he did eventually return and is buried in Canterbury Cathedral, where his helmet, shield and other artefacts are on display. Another reminder of this occasion is the great Crécy window in Gloucester Cathedral. It is the largest stained glass window in existence and takes up almost the whole of the east end of the massive Choir with its soaring fan vaulting. It shows details of all the knights from Gloucestershire who fought at Crécy.

Since that time, the Somme has been fought over many on many occasions. In the south the Santerre Plain possibly takes its name from the Latin, *sancta terra*, or sacred ground. The Romans conquered it and Charlemagne lived there, before the Normans and the English laid claims to it. It was touched many times in the Hundred Years War and was familiar to Henry V. Napoleon's campaign of 1814 ended at Péronne and the Germans first arrived in the war of 1870 before returning in 1914. Rommel passed by Albert in 1940 in pursuit of the British to Dunkirk, before they returned with the Americans in 1944.

Today the local inhabitants are used to seeing the many visitors and pilgrims. I resist the description of 'tourists' being applied in this context as it seems to devalue what happened here to the young men of all nationalities. Inevitably, though, a tourist trade has evolved, albeit somewhat belatedly, as the sleepy French way of life has woken up to the fact that it has something meaningful and valuable in its midst.

Unfortunately, this has not extended, as will be seen, to ensuring that all remaining natural vestiges of the war are preserved. Even as these words are being written, work continues on the 'destruction' of the Redan Ridge mine craters and the last remains of Ridge Redoubt have been bulldozed and topsoiled before being ploughed, all to provide some farmer with a few more euros by way of subsidy. Another example was the siting of a bore hole and pumping station on almost the exact spot where Geoffrey Mallins filmed the explosion of the mine on the Hawthorn Ridge. Nevertheless, despite this destruction of the 'product' they have to sell, the Somme tourist board makes efforts to provide visitors with a welcome and good facilities and a visit to the Tourist Information Office in Albert, near to the Basilique, where they speak English, is worthwhile.

Albert, in recent years, has been improved and brightened up and the square at the west end of the Basilique, while not entirely pedestrianised, now gives priority to pedestrians and has been adorned with attractive bollards, gated areas, flowers and impressive fountains. A museum and souvenir shop which sells battlefield artefacts is sited near the west end of the Basilique. All this has been made possible by the construction some years ago of a by-pass, which has given the busy town a much more peaceful ambiance.

CHAPTER EIGHT

WALKS AND TOURS

In planning these walks due consideration has been given to their starting point, not so much as to the most appropriate location in respect of the battle narrative, but more to ensure the security of the visitor's motor vehicle and property. While crime in rural France is no more a problem, generally, than anywhere else, there has been some systematic targeting of foreign cars, which have been broken into. It is, therefore, entirely up to the reader if a different place is chosen, maybe a little nearer to the 'action'. The whole area is reasonably compact and served by some good tarmac roads and it may be possible to make the 'walks' utilising a vehicle and always have it within reasonable sight. Certainly, if a four wheeled drive is being used there are some excellent tracks in the area to make use of, providing due care is taken and remembering the reputation of Somme mud that is especially sticky and slippery. Even the most innocent looking routes and gradients have claimed their victims. A couple of inches of chalky mud on a hard surface can result in a one hundred per cent loss of traction, not dissimilar to attempting to drive on ice. A skid on this kind of surface can result in a local French farmer being requested to drag a vehicle out of the field, if you can find a willing one!

The safest place to park your vehicle is probably Beaumont Hamel village. There are plenty of places there where it will be close to houses and should not attract undue attention. The same may not be true if it is left unattended for too long outside cemeteries or by memorials where there are usually parking places. That said, a break in is less than likely and most people visit the area without any problem. Follow the unusual precautions and leave any valuables out of sight in the boot.

Walk 1 The German Front Line July 1916

Starting from the cross roads by the school in Beaumont Hamel, follow the single track road, Rue de Montagne, up the hill, past the Memorial to the 51st Highland Division, who recaptured the village in November 1916. This used to be a flag pole, but over the years it has rusted away and now only the base remains with a plaque. This also was in danger of being lost as it was hanging off and at risk of being stolen, a fate some other historical artefacts of its type have suffered in the area in recent years at the hands of 'collectors', but it has now been re-fixed, and the old evergreen spruce trees replaced. The school, like

Turn left along the track towards the German front line position.

many other village schools, is now closed in its own right, but remains operational, equipped as a specialist centre in certain subjects for pupils from various schools to attend. The village, it will be recalled, was in German possession and the front line lay on the outskirts of the village on the left. As you come to the top of the hill there is a small village green and beyond this, on the right, a large group of farm buildings. It was near the entrance to this farm and near the water tower nearby that there were substantial entrances to the subterranean tunnels and galleries that honeycombed the village during the German occupation. A turning along a track to the left marks the start of Watling Street. This was sometimes referred to in the reports and diaries as the Roman Road. A short walk will lead to the Redan Ridge Number 2 Cemetery in the field on the right, but first, after about a hundred metres, you will pass over the site of the German front line. Just before you reach the footpath to the cemetery you will cross the divisional boundary between the 29th Division on the left and the 4th Division to the right. The cemetery stands in what was then No Man's Land, but not far from the German front line on your right as you approach it. Walking on a little further a large copse will be seen on the left. It was immediately in front of this that the German front line ran. If the ground has

Private John Priestley, 1/East Lancs. Lived at Colne in Lancashire. Buried at Redan Ridge Cemetery No.2.

120

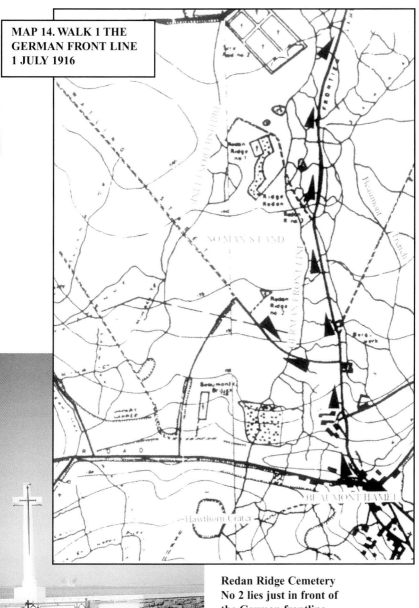

MAP 14. WALK 1 THE
GERMAN FRONT LINE
1 JULY 1916

**Redan Ridge Cemetery
No 2 lies just in front of
the German frontline.**

121

Follow the track to the left to the site of Ridge Redoubt and Redan Ridge Cemetery No.3.

On the site of Ridge Redoubt (Serre Road No 2 Cemetery in background).

been ploughed between the track and the copse, substantial white chalk trench lines may be seen running towards the track on which you are walking. Ahead, on the left, the Sunken Road can be seen and it is possible to visit this at this stage, but it is incorporated into another walk. Watling Street, likewise, is described elsewhere, but it is interesting to note how it ran diagonally across to the British front line and so became a place of refuge, indeed the only natural place of refuge, for the British soldiers in a bare landscape swept by machine-

The destruction of the craters.

gun fire. Return to the metalled road, turn left and continue towards Redan Ridge. In the field on the left, immediately at the side of the road, ran the German front line. In the winter, after ploughing and rain, many hundreds of lead shrapnel balls can be found, lying in the soil staring like the eyes of dead fish, together with fragments of barbed wire and other debris. The British bombardment must have been particularly heavy here.

At the junction of the road and a track that leads to the left you will find Redan Ridge Cemetery Number 3. This is situated a few yards behind the site of the German front line. Continuing up this track, you will pass over the site of Ridge Redoubt. Just recently, a large hole opened up right in the middle of the track, evidence that tunnels still lie deep down on its site. It was not there long, however, as the farmer filled it in with old potatoes! In the appropriate season it is possible to walk in the field on the right and find substantial signs of disturbance. There are large amounts of chalk and flint and other trench debris. The map accompanying this walk was derived from a French map published in the sixties. It will be seen that, at that time, a crater existed in this area, but this has now disappeared and the chalk is probably a remnant of this. Unfortunately, a similar fate has befallen most other traces of the war on the ridge, some of them very recently. These were quite substantial, but for some years the French authorities kindly opened a rubbish dump right next to Redan Ridge Cemetery Number 1. For many years it was an eyesore as they attempted to fill in some of the old craters. It smelt horribly and was infested with rats who were attracted by the dumping of old farm produce, for example small potatoes for which there is no market. Thankfully, this activity ceased and the area was roughly top soiled but attention then turned to what I think were some remains of part of the other mine craters. These were on the right of the path and consisted of a large depression in the ground covered with rough grass and weed but with many shell holes and other prominent disturbance. Initial attempts to re-cultivate the ground proved difficult, even for today's large farm machinery. It was solid with chalk and flint and the tractors seemed to hang at crazy angles on the banking. Eventually, the ground was broken up, some topsoil introduced and levelled. So another small remnant of the Great War disappeared, victim to the quest for a bigger subsidy from the European agricultural bureaucrats. The remaining crater from the aerial photograph of this area used in this book has, as this book is being written, become the next target. It had survived, surrounded by mature trees which date from just after the war period, until 2002. It was filled with stagnant water and was quite forbidding. My dog always showed an unhealthy interest in it and used to look over its quite steep sides as though he was about to jump into it. I vocally discouraged this tendency with some alarm as I am not sure how I

The remains of the crater with Redan Ridge Cemetery No. 1 in the background. (See aerial photograph on page 21).

would have been able to get him out, without some considerable danger of joining him in there. It appeared to be quite deep. Well, Kennedy, the Alsatian, is gone now, the latest British occupant of a grave near the old front line at Beaumont Hamel and so is the crater, well very nearly. My suspicion as to its depth was proven by the fact that attempts to fill it in have not entirely succeeded. I never actually saw the bulldozer working but judging by the track marks and their depth, it was in a similar danger to that of the dog, of sliding into its depths. About that prospect, I have to admit, as far as the bulldozer was concerned, I had ambivalent feelings! My dismay was further enhanced when I realised that I had never taken any photographs of the area. One just does not expect the landscape to change like that. Most of the trees have gone too, a few are left but I expect that these too will soon be fuelling someone's log burner and another landmark relevant to the battlefield visitor will have disappeared entirely.

The cemetery at the summit of the ridge is Redan Ridge Number 1 and this lies in the middle of No Man's Land and was made among the mine craters shown on page 21. As just described these are all but gone now. With your back to the entrance gate it is possible to look across and obtain excellent views of the British positions. To the right, the front line ran behind the two cemeteries near the farm, Serre Road Number 1 and next to it the French Military Cemetery, diagonally approaching the Mailly Maillet to Serre road, crossing it precisely at the left hand corner of the wall of the large British cemetery you can see as you are looking at it now. This is Serre Number 2 British Cemetery. The line then continued round to the left and under the escarpment. It is not difficult, though, to imagine the British troops emerging uphill, over the ridge, to be met by concentrated machine gun fire at fairly close range. It is also easy to see how exposed the troops were to fire from Ridge Redoubt situated just behind the place where you are now standing and why they either veered to the right under the shelter of the escarpment and found Watling Street as a refuge or went sharply to the right and into the congestion at the Quadrilateral. The German front line, meanwhile, was on the right just behind the point where you are standing and as usual dominated the scene of battle. The fields just in that area, to the right, were pasture for cattle and have only been ploughed in recent years. Much debris came to the surface, including many Mills bombs and steel shell cases, mainly British eighteen pounders of the lead ball variety, bearing testimony to the artillery bombardment and the subsequent efforts of the infantry to get into the German lines. At the right time of year, that is after harvest or ploughing, it may be possible to walk directly across this area and pick up the metalled road we were previously walking (or driving) on. A word of warning here, though. The vast majority of farmers in the Somme Département will indulge the battlefield visitor and, as long as the ground is not fenced off, there are no growing crops or there is no notice to the contrary, it is normally permissible to walk on the fields. In this area, though there is a local farmer who falls outside this general rule and I know of several visitors who have been told to get off the land. As different fields are rented or owned by different farms and not always 'ring fenced' as in Britain, it is difficult to know who this man is and which fields are his. My own experience is that one day walking near Redan Ridge Number 3 cemetery, with the dog, a police van suddenly appeared with two gendarmes in it. They stopped about one hundred metres away, had a good look and reversed away. I am convinced someone in Beaumont Hamel had alerted them, possibly mistaking me for an illegal 'shooter' or poacher because of the dog. On another occasion I was on the field by Redan Ridge Number 3 when a farmer's van stopped and the occupant sat and stared at me for at least five minutes, only about fifty yards distant. I was obviously meant to be intimidated. Eventually he drove off as it didn't work! So a little care is needed here and you may prefer to retrace your steps to the point where you left the road to continue.

The road that you are now walking on was either known as Crater Lane or Frontier Lane, depending on which map is consulted. Again it appears on some maps but, as it was probably obliterated, is excluded on others. It runs between the German front line, which was in the field on the left and the second line which was in the field on your right. When the rear of the large British cemetery known as Serre Road Cemetery Number 2, which will be visited later, has been passed, the site of the Quadrilateral is reached. This is located in the field on your left, between the cemetery and the memorial chapel. In the fields to the right, about 200 yards distant, was the site of Boundary Trench, which became Beaumont Trench as it continued to the right towards the village. This was the German third line, which was the area captured and held by the disparate battalions of the 4th Division and recounted

Crater Lane, sometimes known as Frontier Lane, follows the site of the German front line.

by Lieutenant Glover of the 1/Rifle Brigade and Sergeant Cook of the 1/Somerset Light Infantry.

It was here that Drummer Ritchie won his VC, as has also been recorded in Chapter One. He was born in Glasgow and joined the army in 1908 at the age of sixteen. He was wounded at Mons, but returned to the battalion and took part in the Somme attack. He seemed to continue to lead a 'charmed life' and was again wounded in 1917. Before the end of the war he was twice wounded again and gassed twice. He nevertheless continued his career in the army until 1929. He worked as a recruiting officer for the army in a Glasgow school. He died in 1965 aged 72

It may be possible to walk across the field and get on to the actual site from here, but there is another walk which will take you nearer the place from another direction. All the ground in this area was strongly disputed on 1 July, before, as we have seen, being given up by the British, who only managed to retain the portion of ground between Crater Lane and the Mailly-Serre road, the actual Quadrilateral, before withdrawing altogether. It may be possible from this position to see Munich Trench Cemetery on the right, which is near to the point where the troops made their furthest advance here on 1 July. Mature trees in the cemetery have recently been replaced, so it is not as easy as it used to be, but it may be possible to spot the tops of the new ones and the cross of sacrifice, weather and growing crops permitting, in the distance.

Drummer W Ritchie VC.

As the end of the single track road is reached, Serre Road Cemetery Number One will be seen opposite, but before turning our attentions to that, look to the right where a banking and line of trees along the right hand edge of a field almost meet the track. This was the end of a large German communication trench known as Ten Tree Alley, which ran all the way back behind the German lines nearly as far as Miraumont. We will look at this trench again as part of another walk. To return to the point we have now reached on this walk, the German front line crossed

128

the main road at exactly the point where the single track joins it. The farm on the right must stand on the site. A further word of warning here. There has been some confrontations here with one of the occupants of the farm and visitors in the past. Access to the cemeteries signposted at the side of the farm has been disputed. This went as far as individuals being assaulted and vehicles being attacked. Fortunately, with the assistance of the Gendarmes and support of the Commonwealth War Graves Commission, who have an important interest here, matters seem to have been settled. There are, though, now red warning signs about causing obstruction on the track to the Sheffield Memorial Park, which should be taken seriously. The park itself is not part of the remit of this book so we can leave it aside.

The British Front Line

Serre Road Cemetery Number One situated at the junction of the 31st and 4th Divisions, was started as a battlefield cemetery and then expanded as a concentration cemetery subsequently. At the rear, which is close to the site of the British front line, graves from both divisions can be found; included from the 4th Division are the 6/Warwicks, 8/Warwicks, 2/Essex, 1/Rifle Brigade and the King's Own Lancasters. It was here that survivors of the Leeds and Bradford 'Pals' made

Serre Road No.1 Cemetery. It was here that the Bradford 'Pals' survivors made regular pilgrimages.

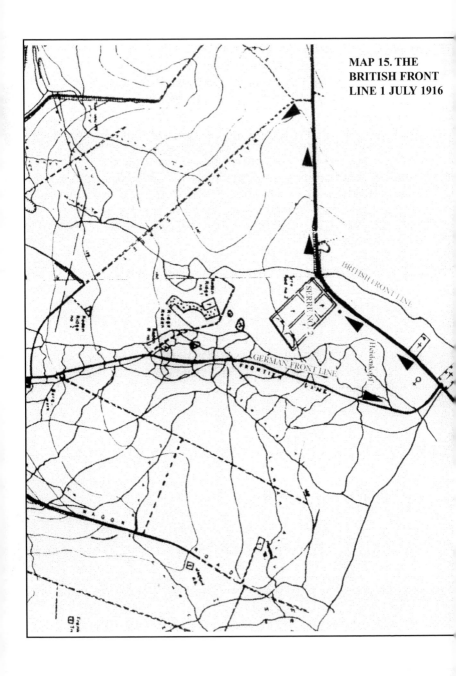

MAP 15. THE
BRITISH FRONT
LINE 1 JULY 1916

The Last Parade. This picture was taken on the very last time the Bradford 'Pals' made the trip.

regular 'reunions', the last of which was featured on television some years ago and which clearly illustrated the grief still experienced by the ageing survivors.

The French National Cemetery which lies close by has an interesting history and was created from the battles here in 1915, before the British took over this sector. When the battlefields were being cleared by the British, any remains of the French soldiers were buried separately and as remains were found further afield, so they were brought here to be buried. In all there are about eight hundred graves now, but the cemetery was maintained by the Imperial War Graves Commission until 1933, after which the French took it over. The French regiments that fought here included the 233rd and 243rd

Valentine Braithwaite was educated at Winchester College and went on to Sandhurst. He was commissioned in the 1/Somerset Light Infantry in August 1914 and went to France the following month. At the beginning of 1915 he was awarded the Military Cross for gallant conduct at Mons and was Mentioned in Despatches. He went to the Dardanelles as ADC to the Chief of the General Staff and was again mentioned in Despatches. In 1916 he resigned his appointment as ADC and rejoined his battalion in France. He was a platoon commander on the 1 July and was last seen in the Quadrilateral encouraging his men forward. His body was never identified for burial.

His father bought the plot of land in the Quadrilateral where his son was last seen and erected the memorial cross. Some years later when the whole field was sold it was discovered that the wrong piece of land had been conveyed to the Braithwaites and they actually owned a piece of ground in Serre No 2 cemetery. It took some time to sort it all out but eventually the new owner allowed the cross and the plot to be re sited near to the road side where it stands today.

Memorial to Lieutenant V A Braithwaite MC. Site of the Quadrilateral in background.

and the 327th. Most of the men involved were locally recruited and fought with fanatical courage which moved the German commander to make a fine tribute to their achievement in holding up the Germans. The British front line ran in the field behind the French cemetery, coming diagonally towards the road which it crossed at the right hand corner of the next cemetery among this cluster, Serre Number 2. In this area a glance at the map will show that the 8th Royal Warwicks were assembled in the field on the right, opposite the Quadrilateral. This was sited in the field to the left of Serre Number 2. The road was the base of this position and was from where the remnants of the 4th Division retired on 1 July. Three small British mines had

The French cemetery and memorial chapel.

previously been exploded here, but, as we have seen the position was left virtually undefended and the German mine, much bigger, exploded without its desired effect on the British. Unusually, there is little evidence today of all this activity and disturbance, which must have been considerable. The obvious reason for this is that it has been subsequently topsoiled, as nothing would grow on chalk and flint and this was a practice carried on for many years after the war, as the area was reclaimed. Several walks across the site has not revealed anything other than the odd nose cone or a few live mills bombs, which seems ironic as we have already learnt how desperately short in supply these were on 1 July 1916. A bit further along this field, behind the cemetery, I did find a most interesting belt buckle. Identification has proved to be difficult, but it is possibly from a German chaplain as it has two crossed swords on which is superimposed a bishop's mitre.

133

Captain Charles E Baird, Seaforth Highlanders. Killed 1 July 1916 and buried in Serre Road Number 2.

The chapel stands opposite the French cemetery and I have only known it to be open on the anniversary of the battle in June, when a memorial service is held and invited guests are offered a *Vin d'Honnuer* afterwards at the farm previously mentioned. There are two plaques on the chapel, one to the chaplain to the French regiments here and the other a brief dedication in German to the 'BRIR 1'. RIR stands for Reserve Infantry Regiment, but it is not known for sure what the B stands for.

On the extreme left of Serre Road Cemetery Number 2 is a special memorial cross to the memory of Second Lieutenant V A Braithwaite MC, 1st Somerset Light Infantry, who was killed near here on 1 July, probably in the Quadrilateral. His father, Lieutenant General W Braithwaite, was a corps commander.

Serre Road Cemetery Number 2 is the largest cemetery on the Somme battlefields with 7,139 graves, but nearly 5,000 are unidentified. Originally less than 500 were buried here in 1917, but by 1922 many bodies had been brought here from many parts of the battlefields. This concentration continued until 1934, when the present capacity was reached. The ground slopes up and away from the roadside and it is a sobering sight to see the rows and rows of soldiers graves disappearing into the distance.

One of the first visits here by a relative was made before the end of the war in 1918 and we have been left an interesting account of this pilgrimage.

Second Lieutenant Henry Lionel Field, 6th Royal Warwicks. Killed 1 July 1916 and buried in Serre Road Number 2.
Above the shot-blown trench he stands.
Tall and thin against the sky;
His thin white face and thin white hands,
Are the signs his people know him by.
His soldier's coat is silver barred
And on his head the well-known crest.
Above the shot-blown trench he stands.
The bright escutcheon on his breast,
and traced in silver bone for bone
The likeness of a skeleton.
H L Field

Colonel W R Ludlow had been a commanding officer of a battalion in the Warwickshire Regiment. His son had followed in his father's footsteps and had accepted a commission in the same regiment. On 1 July he had been a company commander, leading his men of the 1/8th Battalion into the attack, and was seen smoking a cigarette and urging his men forward in the German front line trenches. After that he was not

Serre Road No 2.

seen again.

In March 1918 the Germans were preparing for a major offensive that was to recapture all of the ground so painfully won by the Allies in almost two years of fighting. However, on 11 March all this was still to come and attempts were still being made to get back to normal by many of the local population. Into all this came

Headstones in Serre Road Cemetery Number 2, original graves from 1 July form the centre piece.

Captain M Partridge, 2/ Lancashire Fusiliers, killed in action 1 July. Among those buried in Serre Road Number 2.

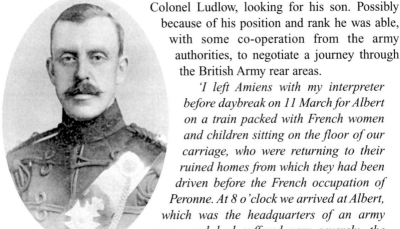

Colonel W R Ludlow

Captain S W Ludlow, commanded A Company, 8/Royal Warwickshire Regiment, is buried in Serre Road No 2.

Colonel Ludlow, looking for his son. Possibly because of his position and rank he was able, with some co-operation from the army authorities, to negotiate a journey through the British Army rear areas.

'I left Amiens with my interpreter before daybreak on 11 March for Albert on a train packed with French women and children sitting on the floor of our carriage, who were returning to their ruined homes from which they had been driven before the French occupation of Peronne. At 8 o'clock we arrived at Albert, which was the headquarters of an army corps, and had suffered very severely, the town being partly in ruins and the magnificent statue of the Virgin and Child hanging tragically down from the spire of the cathedral. The corps headquarters placed every facility for my inspection on explaining my errand and showing the sketch of the spot where my son fell, and we were at once furnished with large scale maps showing the line of the British and Hun trenches as they existed in 1916. From there we went to the Graves Registration Department and discussed the matter thoroughly with the officers in charge, who showed us maps on the wall over which they worked, covering a distance of about eighteen miles long and twenty miles wide. It did not include the Serre and Beaumont Hamel areas and a good many others. But they had already located many thousands of graves and made a large number of cemeteries. This gives some faint idea of the awful losses which have taken place in the blood stained fields of the Somme.

A Scene of Desolation

Later on in the morning, through the kindness of the Graves Registration Department, a motor and a guide were placed at our disposal, and after a few miles we got beyond the cultivated area to the old battlefield of Beaumont Hamel, Serre, *Auchenvilliers* (Auchonvillers), *Hébuterne*, *Foncvilliers* (Foncquevillers) *and Goumercourt* (Gommecourt). *These were only names on the map, as there is nothing to denote that they have ever been occupied as human habitations. Having located the village of Serre we worked our way back along the road south to the point where the old British line of 1916 crossed. When I visited the spot on 12 March, beyond this village of which only the outside walls of a few houses remained standing, the country was a complete waste, a series of rolling plains covered with thick, coarse, brown grass, every tree, hedge and pollard had disappeared, and only mounds covered with grass showed where villages had been. A few cabbages or broccoli struggled through the matted surface, and stumps of apple trees denoted what had once been garden and flourishing orchards. The trenches were grown over or had fallen in, or had filled with water in places, while the whole area was a mass of old shell holes. It was here that the 8th Battalion went into the German lines.*

Relics of the Battlefield

In the subsequent fighting and the German retreat from Serre, the whole country has been so badly shelled that it was extremely difficult to get about the area. This part of the field had not been fully explored, and here and there one came across piles of equipment, coats and tunics, rusty rifles, bayonets and frogs, bully beef tins not opened, shells, hand grenades, and boxes of Mills bombs unopened, and all the usual debris of the battlefield. Along the line occupied by 11 Brigade there were the remains of Huns' skulls and bones and shrapnel helmets in all directions. A number of officers' tin hats were lying about and one grave with a cross upon it and no inscription had a tin hat attached to it. One grave was marked by a harrow but the majority of them were hidden by the tall, rank grass or were destroyed by subsequent shell fire. I sat on the edge of a shell hole opposite to the German position in No Man's Land, and wondered how it was possible that any troops in the world could attack such a position in broad daylight on a lovely July morning. From careful investigation it was obvious that the wire had not been completely destroyed. There was not sufficient cover for a mouse except that which was afforded by shell holes in moving forward to the attack. Anyone would feel very proud and sad at the same time that two splendid battalions, which I had once had the honour of commanding, should have behaved so splendidly and had

On the site of the old British line as it crossed Watling Steet. The German line is identified by the clump of trees (the old craters) and Redan Ridge Cemetery No 3. No troops got past this right-hand side of the ridge on 1 July and the ground was covered with the dead and wounded.

been attached to the immortal brigade of regulars which formed the storming troops on that wonderful day. Within the old German lines is the Serre Road Cemetery No 1, a little square of about one acre, crowded with graves of our gallant regiments. A great number of these were nameless and inscribed to an unknown British Officer or an unknown British Soldier, but there were a great many names of old friends in the rank and file, although I could find very few officers.

Along Watling Street.

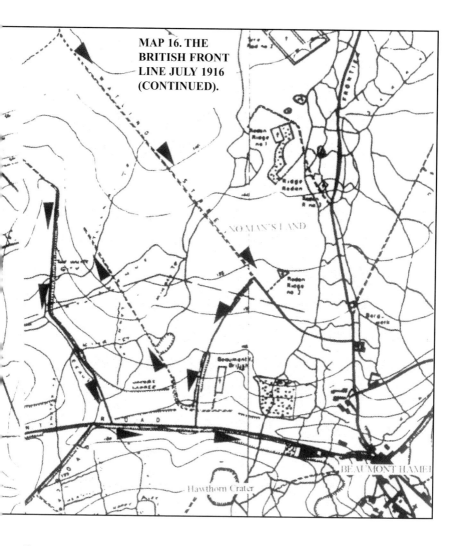

MAP 16. THE
BRITISH FRONT
LINE JULY 1916
(CONTINUED).

*About 100 yards to the right of Serre Road Cemetery No 1 was a very
fine stone obelisk with a bronze inscription and bronze chains and
posts round it, bearing the following inscription in French 'To the
brave soldiers of the 242nd Regiment who died for their Country, June
15th 1915' and the thought ran through my mind that my friends in
Birmingham might wish to see a similar suitable memorial to the 6th
and 8th Battalions, which might be erected after the war. On a slight
rise in the ground to the west of the cemetery was a wooden cross to
an officer of the Somerset Light Infantry, bearing the following*

inscription 'God buried him and no man knows of his sepulchre, 1st July 1916'.

Permanent Tombstones

Serre Road Cemetery No 2 lies about 300 yards in front of the old line on the east of the road, and consists mainly of graves of the officers and ranks and file of 11 Brigade. As part of the battlefield has not been thoroughly examined or cleared, there are only approximately one tenth of the number who fell in that battle who had been identified and buried within the area of the cemeteries and now it will be soon even more difficult to trace their graves. The many hours I was on the battlefield I never saw a single sign of life of any kind or description, or traffic, nor were there any signs of large bodies of troops anywhere within the immediate neighbourhood. On arrival again at Albert, the Graves Registration staff promised to prosecute the search but of course this is now impossible. They also showed us a book of designs which the army is getting out for permanent tombstones to replace the wooden crosses which were very simple and beautiful, and the cost will be kept down so that people with very modest means may have a permanent memorial to their dear ones.

So Colonel Ludlow did not find his son, at least on that occasion. He was subsequently found, and is now buried in Serre Road Cemetery Number 2 and, perhaps, the Colonel was able to make the journey again after the war to visit the grave.

Continue your walk

Continue along the road to Mailly-Maillet, taking care to avoid the traffic, which is not heavy but travels at considerable speed when it does come, and always in the other direction than we are used to in the British Isles. Just where the road bears to the right, the British front line is crossed. This road was the divide between the attacking battalions here. On the right the 6/Warwicks were following their namesakes, while on the left the 1/Rifle Brigade occupied the ground and were followed by the 1/Somerset Light Infantry. Further on, just where the 1/King's Own were astride the road in support, there is a single track road on the left which you should take. If you are supplementing this walk with the use of a vehicle, do not worry too much about the no entry sign. This is there to prevent motorists taking a short cut to Auchonvillers and causing a traffic jam with agricultural vehicles. If there is nothing about it is possible to drive the short distance to where a track leads off to the left and park there. Before

BEAUMONT CHURCH

HAWTHORN CRATER

German Front Line

The junction of Watling Street and the Sunken Road. It was here that the patrol of the 1/Royal Warwicks, led by Lieutenant Waters, was stopped by machine gun fire.

that, however, look ahead down the main road and where it rises up and bears left is where the 2/Essex were also in support. The group of farm buildings in the distance is where the 2/Duke of Wellington's were in reserve. The existence of this road probably accounts for their rapid advance when called into the attack and the failure of the order to halt their advance. At that time these buildings were the site of a sugar refinery.

To return to the track, this is the other end of Watling Street and will take you back to Beaumont Hamel and is normally passable by four wheeled drive vehicles too. In my experience it is quite difficult to estimate distances when there are no points of reference, and the first thing you will notice is that the fields are quite open. To indicate that the front line was about two hundred yards away may not be too helpful unless it is possible to pace it out, which it may be, of course. As we continue along the track, we have now come round to the rear of the British positions. After about 500 metres the positions where the right flank of the 1/Somersets and left flank of the 2/Seaforths met will be reached. Again the track was the precise dividing line, but there is no reference point to mark the actual position. Further on, the left flank of the 1/Hampshires straddled the track, but the most substantial portion of their ground lay in the fields to the right. Finally, as we approach the point where the track crossed No Man's Land, the 1/East Lancs held a long narrow section of front line trench extending on both sides of Watling Street. To complete the picture along the track just negotiated try and imagine the wounded and the work of those charged with the task of assisting them. Reports state that there where some terrible scenes along this now peaceful and rural lane, and the suffering and fear must be beyond comprehension. On the left, it will have been observed that the site of Ridge Redoubt dominated the landscape and, as now, there was not a scrap of natural cover, only shell holes to hide in and wait, hopefully, for a chance to drag a wounded body back to a safer place. To complete this walk, continue straight on, crossing No Man's Land. The right turn will take you down to the sunken road and the boundary with the 29th Division, but this will be visited in another walk.

The Sunken Road today.

It was to this position, the junction of the two tracks, that the patrol of the 1/Warwicks, A Company, led Lieutenant Waters reached before being driven back by machine gun fire, the last act on the evening of 1 July before the attack was abandoned. As will be seen this was quite close to the German front line, which is crossed again before the village of Beaumont Hamel is reached.

Betrayal

Before we leave this side of the Redan Ridge and move on to the area of the November battles let us briefly look back to the beginning of the year. Much has already been written on this topic, but to ignore it would not be justified.

In January 1916 a young soldier of the 9/Royal Irish Rifles was found to be missing from the trenches they were holding on Redan Ridge. His name was James Crozier and by coincidence carried the same name as the battalion commander. The connection went further, as when James went to enlist in Belfast, his mother turned up and told the recruiting officer that he was only seventeen and was about to drag him away. Lieutenant Colonel F P Crozier, as he subsequently became, intervened and persuaded the woman to relent, offering to look after his namesake personally.

The young Crozier was found wandering around an ammunition dump in the rear area and was escorted back to divisional headquarters in Mailly Maillet. A subsequent Court Martial was held and he was quickly found guilty, offering no defence other than that he was disorientated, his body was painful and he could not remember anything. He was sentenced to be shot but with a recommendation for mercy. However, the sentence was confirmed by Sir Douglas Haig, perhaps largely because of the comments of Lieutenant Colonel Crozier.

On the night of 26/27 February, James was plied with liquor, and at 7 o'clock in the morning, unable to stand and probably unaware what was happening to him, was taken out into the snow, tied to a chair and shot. The time was recorded as 7.05 am.

The only witnesses were the firing party and the officer in charge, who had been forced to spend the previous evening with his commanding officer, allegedly to prevent him from avoiding the ordeal by getting drunk himself. It is not known whether a padre was present. While the battalion paraded on the other side of the high wall, out of sight but within earshot of the proceedings, Lieutenant Colonel Crozier mounted upon his horse, rode on to the top of a soil bank and observed his handiwork over the top of the wall. James Crozier was originally buried where he was executed, but he was later exhumed and now lies in the Sucrerie Military Cemetery.

The location of James Crozier's demise can be found near the lovely little church in the village. There is a high red bricked wall on the road to Englebelmer and it was here that his battalion paraded. This was the perimeter wall of the chateau that once stood here but was destroyed in the revolution. Just opposite the church there is a recreation area and it is possible to walk behind the wall. Nearby is the only remains of the chateau, a little mortuary chapel, for which local residents are attempting to raise funds to preserve. I have wondered whether that was where the unfortunate boy spent his last hours.

Walk 2

This walk starts at the memorial to the 8/Argyll and Sutherland Highlanders, which is situated at the well known Sunken Road close to Beaumont Hamel British Cemetery. Leaving Beaumont Hamel on the Auchonvillers road, this will be seen on the right hand side. The whole area here is very interesting and one of the most frequented on the Somme battlefields. Access to the crater on Hawthorn Ridge can be found on the left just before the signpost to the cemetery on the right. The Celtic cross memorial is the largest to a single battalion, bigger than most divisional memorials. The activities of the Lancashire Fusiliers in the Sunken Road, filmed by Geoffrey Mallins, are well documented. No description is better, in my opinion, than in the book

Past the A & S memorial is where the British front line crossed.

The Lancashire Fusiliers (29th Division) assemble for the 1 July attack, near the White City.

The remains of the dugouts can be found in the banking today.

My Bit, by George Ashurst. He was here at the time and survived going over the top towards the wood and ran back later unscathed. He and his comrades held the position overnight, and George helped man a Lewis gun position at the bottom of the road, near where the path to the cemetery starts. Anyone not familiar with this is strongly recommended to read it.

There were trench mortar positions in the lane and for many years some of the entrances were still visible. I once met a visitor there who told me he had crawled in to one of these but had become stuck and only by being pulled out by a rope and some additional manpower got him free, but it gave him a nasty shock. The entrances are now gone, although it took about eighty-five years for someone to get round to it. This was prompted by a large hole appearing in the field on the right, just on top of the bank. What appears to have occurred is that when the open shafts of the mortar positions were filled in they were boarded with railway sleepers, then the soil put on top. This arrangement supported the horses and tractors over the years until the sleepers rotted away. The depth of the hole suggests that the sleepers were quite near the surface and, what is more, the persons undertaking this operation did not bother to clear out the dugout beforehand. There were numerous 'toffee apples', full of explosive, not armed, but with the brass plug still in place. More interestingly, there were complete boxes of Newton's fuses, small bundles of explosive and fulmanite of mercury detonators all neatly arranged inside in egg rack type formation, along with all the other bits and pieces needed to arm these mortars. There were also army instruction booklets in perfect condition. It needed a ladder to get into the hole and I resisted the invitation as the sides looked unstable. I did eventually succumb, though, but only because I found a hedgehog had fallen in and could not get out!

The full investigation was left to a local Frenchman I contacted, who was more used to this type of challenge. He also found, deep in the chalk, a tunnel running parallel to the lane. There were junctions turning to the left, towards the lane but nothing running forward in the direction of the German front line. A French gardener, though, who has many years service with the Commonwealth War Graves Commission, told me that a tunnel exit was, for many years, visible in the bank on the left just beyond the Beaumont Hamel British Cemetery wall. It was used to deposit rubbish from the cemetery and is now completely filled up. It must have started from the sunken road, and was probably dug for the November attack from here. No doubt the vestiges of its construction are still there under the field. Just beyond the end of the trees and bushes was the divisional boundary between the 4th Division and the 29th Division. Before we retrace our steps and continue in another direction, a final anecdote about the Sunken Road. There are accounts telling of how the dead were buried in the lane and its banking. Not all were found after the war, it seems, for some British visitors recently claimed to have found a skeleton showing in the track. While they certainly found one, this could not have been in the track.

The British mine on Hawthorn Ridge explodes 1 July 1916 fired controversially ten minutes before the infantry assault began.

It is not long ago that this track which is of compacted chalk and flint was resurfaced with about a foot of similar material. What I suspect happened is that they were digging illegally nearby and concocted the story for the authorities.

Return to the memorial and turn to the right and follow the path round. On the edge of the embankment and the field half left ahead are the remains of a lookout post. It used to be quite complete and it was possible to stand in its semi circular construction and imagine the sand bags on top and the Hawthorn mine going up at close quarters. As with many remnants of interest the farmer has partly destroyed this to try and get a bit more subsidy and it may well be gone altogether soon.

Continue up the track and you are now in No Man's Land walking towards the British front line. Remember that the Sunken Road was in No Man's Land. You are soon in the 4th Division sector and crossing the ground occupied by the 1/East Lancs and then the 1st Hampshires. On the map, this track is shown as terminating near to a steep banking half left ahead. In reality the farmer sometimes ploughs this at varying distances, so if substantial crops are growing there may be a problem.

If so, it is best to find your way to the banking by turning left where it seems most promising at the time. The ground on which the 2/Seaforths formed up is close by and when the bank is finally reached walk along the top until a suitable place to descend is found. This is most likely to be where the substantial track you can see below the embankment turns to the left. This area was the original White City. I say original because the area extending back along the track, under the embankment, is generally referred to by this name and became named as such by adoption. Most of the battalions mentioned had headquarters here. The 2/Seaforths' ground was bit further on from where the track turns to the left, but we will walk along the track back under the embankment. Here many remains of tunnels, shelters and dugouts can be seen and the area where the 2/R Dublins were in support is reached. This was mainly under the embankment and in the field on the right, but also extended on top of the banking and behind the 1/Hampshires. There is a quarry on the left and this is often reported as being the site of battalion headquarters and so is likely to have been utilised by the 2/R Dublins. There was also a large Royal Engineers dump and after the war a cemetery was made here, but it was concentrated later. Indeed, the whole area was a mass of activity and it is easy to imagine the feverish attempts to assist the wounded and dying made by the Royal Army Medical Corps and the brave work of the stretcher bearers. Many ambulances lurched along the track back in the direction of Mailly Maillet, probably with the less severely wounded and, as darkness fell, those trapped out in No Man's Land returned, scrambling down the steep sandbagged banking and into comparative safety. The excavations into the bank produced large amounts of chalk which was subsequently spread about and, therefore, gave the area its name. Fortunately, the area was filmed and photographed, so we have some record, but these, of course, would be strictly censored or even staged. It would not be allowed to show pictures of what we know really happened here.

Looking to the right a small valley or re-entrant will be seen with banking on each side. This was the site of 4th Avenue and 5th Avenue trenches. These were large communication trenches and probably guided the 1/East Lancs and the 1/Hampshires to their positions on the evening of 30 June. It was in this area to the right that a few years ago some British visitors discovered the body of a New Zealand soldier. The field had been deeply ploughed and there had been heavy rain. He was probably lying face down, maybe as he fell. The plough came along precisely in the same direction and turned him over, in the

Site of sub-station

Mallins's picture of the Lancashire Fusiliers moving up.

The same place (circa 1990). The old trench spoil has been bulldozed. Note the hedge lines on the far side of the Beaumont-Auchonvillers road which mark the old British front line, now also bulldozed.

process only damaging his skull. The rain then washed him out, lying on his back on the surface. When a body is found, the gendarmes are called, the local mayor attends and the landowner or tenant too. An 'inquest' is held and the origin of the body decided, that is, whether it is a soldier at which point the appropriate authorities are called. Sometimes they are already there as it is the war graves workers that find it. This soldier had all his equipment with him and he was found to have come from Auckland, but his name tags had long disintegrated. He was buried at Terlincthun Cemetery near Boulogne, where there is a plot where all recovered bodies were taken. Now this practice has

BRITISH FRONT LINE

◄ Beaumont Auchonvillers ►

Lancashire Fusiliers crawling out into No Man's Land 1 July 1916.

The same place today.

been discontinued and those found are buried in the nearest appropriate cemetery.

Our man would have died in 1918 when the New Zealand forces drove the Germans back through this area following their advance in March of that year. If my theory is right, then he was facing the direction of the advance.

As we continue along the track we leave the 4th Division sector and move into the 29th Division area. It was here that Mallins filmed the famous sequence of Lancashire Fusiliers coming up the trench and turning left, ostensibly up to the front line on 1 July. The authenticity of this is in doubt and it was probably staged before that day but, nonetheless, provides an interesting picture of the area and the reality, for all that, is hardly diminished. It was shot at the junction of King Street and Esau's Way. This location can be found by looking for the tallest tree that stands among some bushes on top of the bank. I have calculated this by a simple bit of map reading to be the place and it is about 250 meters from the Beaumont road. If someone has chopped the tree down, which is perfectly possible, then climb on the bank and look for the stump! Stand and look in the direction that Mallins filmed

'Hunched figures retreated before the German machine guns.' Possibly the sudden retirement recorded in the diary of the Lancashire Fusiliers at 9.45 am, 1 July 1916.

Cattle now graze peacefully above the Beaumont road.

Bear right up the track towards Beaumont Trench.

and the Old Beaumont road can be seen, but without the Poplar trees (the stumps are still in the bank) and the site of the old British frontline in the field beside it. This too, until a few years ago, survived with some notable remains, but has since been ploughed up, but the location is unmistakable. Walking on it will be seen that the 'soil' along the last part of the track is very chalky. This is because the field on the right was pasture until recent years. Originally large mounds of trench spoil covered the area which had grassed over and on which cattle grazed.

On the site where the Beaumont Trench crossed the track.

When it was ploughed, vast quantities of war debris appeared, rusting equipment, explosives, buckles, buttons, coins – too much to mention. It was soon cleared by 'field walkers', so there is not much chance of a 'find'.

Where the escarpment on the left turns to the left a concrete hut will be seen. This was thoughtfully placed there right on the old front line and houses an electric pump that sucks up water from a bore hole. This is very recent and miles of water pipes were laid under the fields to carry it. Just on the corner there were some good examples of British dugouts, overgrown but unmistakably rectangular. All that would have been needed was some sandbags and corrugated iron to get a reasonable reconstruction. However, these were bulldozed. The front line ran up the bank to the left and the water pipe commenced its journey right along its site in the field above. This was interesting as it exposed a length of the original trench complete with revetting, rusting corrugated iron and wooden stakes. I decided that there was nothing else to be found, not even a rusted water bottle. However, I was wrong. Two visitors staying at my home, which was situated close-by, went to have a look. They were not gone long because of the intense cold, but in a short time they returned with a good example of an Irish regimental cap badge!

The front line on the right crossed the field towards the road and where there is a small electric sub-station at the bottom of the Old Beaumont road, which is the track you will see, then turned half left and ran up the field to the left of the track. Until a few years ago this area was a storage area for farm equipment and produce and was surrounded by scrub and bushes in which were the remains of the old trench. When it was bulldozed and ploughed much trench debris came to light. The French must have put up a strong fight here as the most common item was spent Lebel cartridges. To see what it was like on 1 July, have a look at the official film, *The Battle of the Somme*. There is a sequence showing the attack here as it took place. Soldiers come over the top of the trench, some appear to be hit and fall. Others run down towards the top of the bank above the road, probably in an attempt to find 'dead' ground, away from the machine gun fire These men would have belonged the 29th Division, either to the 1/Lancashire Fusiliers, who were first across, or the 16/Middlesex, who followed them and were assembled in the field behind you either side of the Beaumont road, and right across beyond where the house and the poplar trees stand almost as far as you can see towards Auchonvillers.

Walk past the pumping station for about twenty metres. You are now within a few paces of the site, raised up in the banking, of the position occupied by Geoffrey Mallins when he filmed the explosion of the Hawthorn Crater and the events just described. I have deduced this from still photographs showing his position in relation to the Old Beaumont road, and from there it is a simple bit of visual alignment. If desired it is possible to climb the bank and continue along the top. In the field on the left was the divisional boundary between the 29th and the 4th Divisions, about 250 yards distant. On the right, good views of the crater are obtained and it is interesting to consider that when it was blown many reports stated that the earth shook, and one man reportedly had his leg broken by the aftershock. He had been bracing his leg against the side of the trench. However, on Mallins film, the camera remains quite steady as it explodes, and does not move at all. Whether you are on the top of the bank or have taken the easier route along the bottom, the remains of substantial excavations will be seen. These were forward trenches, saps and observation bunkers, many with spy holes, through which the British watched their adversary.

The end of the walk is now reached at the Sunken Road and if you wish to visit the crater it is possible to do so by taking the track previously mentioned in the Beaumont road. Good views can be obtained of the Redan Ridge, but if you wish to descend into the crater, it is better to walk all the way round to the side facing the village, until a fence is encountered. Immediately to the left there is normally a gap and a relatively gentle slope to negotiate, but it may be overgrown with stinging nettles in the summer!

In recent years, two Frenchmen found the remains of a German soldier in the crater, but I do not think this was reported. I was lucky to find a complete German helmet on the lip of the crater where the bank was crumbling away.

Returning to the road, walk back to Beaumont village. As you pass the track on the left that is the entrance to the Sunken Road and Beaumont Hamel Military Cemetery, note the ditch in the field just on the left that runs parallel to the road. There has been some speculation as to whether this is an old trench. It features in the book *My Bit* by George Ashhurst, previously mentioned. George recalls how a German patrol crawled up the ditch on the morning of 2 July to find out what the situation was in the Sunken Road and were fired on by George and his Lewis gun crew. The ditch may well be the remnant of a forward sap and could have been dug by the Germans from their front line which was situated about 120 yards away in front of Beaumont village. The line ran along the front of the small wood on the left as you continue and there are shell holes and other signs of disturbance still remaining in there. The little copse on the right a bit further on has similar features and is owned by the people who live at the first house on the left, whose dwelling is built on the site of the old German second line trench.

Walk 3. The November Battles

The site of the British front line for the November attacks was largely the same position as that of 1 July. In the intervening period nothing of note had taken place in this sector, all the activity, especially in September, had occurred around Thiepval, further south of the Ancre River. The only attacks on the immediate north bank in front of Hamel village had been in support of that action.

In the meantime the line had been improved, as far as weather conditions allowed. It was straightened and strengthened, for example,

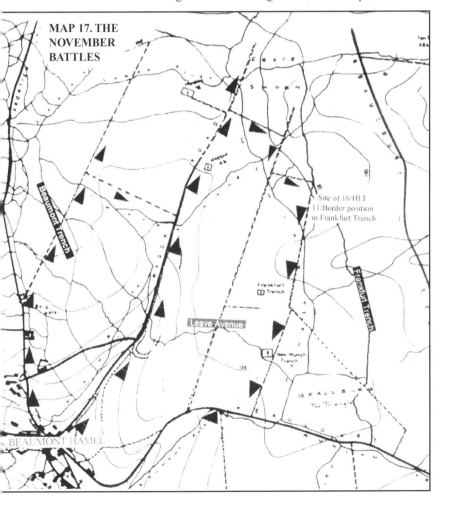

MAP 17. THE
NOVEMBER
BATTLES

Site of 16/HLI 11/Border position in Frankfurt Trench

Beaumont Trench

Frankfurt Trench

Frankfurt Trench

Leave Avenue

New Munich Trench

BEAUMONT HAMEL

where the original line crossed the Auchonvillers-Beaumont road near the water pumping station, this position was now brought forward to the Sunken Road and became part of the front line known as Hunter's Avenue. For the most part, however, the line remained static and, therefore, we can refer to the part of the book that covers this, except, of course, to remember that the conditions for the two attacks were very different. In July the ground was firm under foot and covered with wild grass, weeds and wild flowers, through which the men had peered for a sight of their objective and, perhaps, the enemy. In November the conditions were, as we know, quite appalling and it was difficult to even stand up and avoid slipping deep into the mud.

We can start our tour of the November battlefield, once again, at Beaumont Hamel village. I have constructed the route as a walk but it is possible to visit some of the areas by car. For example, all the cemeteries have a tarmac road to reach them, except Munich Trench, to which it an easy walk from where the road becomes a rough track. The problem is that they are narrow and there is no turning space. It may be necessary to reverse out quite a long way. If, however, the ground is dry or frozen and firm it is possible to turn round by reversing on to the fields, in many places, but extreme care needs to be exercised to avoid becoming stuck in the mud. There are many tracks and paths that cross the area, so it is easy to get right on to the ground described in the battle narrative. At certain times of the year, when there are no crops growing, it may be possible to walk on the fields and take short cuts or, if desired, reach the positions described by a different route altogether.

It will be recalled that on 13 November, the 2/HLI and the 24/Royal Fusiliers led the attack of the 2nd Division and reached their objective, Beaumont Trench, albeit with many casualties. Here they were to be 'leap frogged' by the following up battalions and the advance continued. It is possible to get into the vicinity of Beaumont Trench by taking the Rue de Montagne from the 51st Division flagpole, as we did in the previous walk of the British frontline, as far as the water tower on the right at the top of the hill. Here a track leads off to the right and by walking along this you will be in the area where the trench existed. After about two hundred yards the point is reached where it crossed the track. Standing on the track and facing ahead the trench came from a half left direction and continued at a similar angle behind you. Ahead of you to the left is the area where Drummer Ritchie won his VC and the mixed force of troops held on grimly to their modest gains on July 1. The majority of the 2/HLI and 24/Royal Fusiliers would also have been dug in ahead of you on 13 November. It will be noted that the area is quite flat and would have been completely devoid of any cover. It is possible to walk quite a long way on this track although it ultimately finishes in a dead end not far from Ten Tree Alley. Before that a turning on the right is reached and this will take you into some of the areas covered by this walk, however I have constructed the walk to recommence from the 51st Division Memorial, so as not to miss one or two interesting things in Wagon road, but the choice is yours.

Walk further on along this track, anyway, for about 250 yards and the place where one of some literary associations with this part of the Somme Battlefields will be very close. As far as I have been able to ascertain, the death of Lance-Sergeant H H Munro occurred somewhere close by in the area to your left. Munro was better known as the author 'Saki'. It is widely reported that while involved in holding the defensive flank near the Quadrilateral with the 22/Royal Fusiliers, already referred to, his last words were, 'Put that bloody cigarette out'. The inference is that he was then shot by the sniper who had seen the culprit light up. However, it is almost certain that he was killed by shell fire.

Back at the flagpole in Beaumont, look for the green Commonwealth War Graves signs to Waggon Road and Munich Trench cemeteries (note the different spelling of Waggon on the signs). This part of Wagon Road, as we proceed, was, of course, in the 51st Division sector and on the right as we proceed a large quarry will be seen. It was in this location that there were many entrances to the subterranean tunnels that existed under the village and that the Germans utilised to turn the village into a fortress. The origin of these tunnels are a natural phenomenon, caused by the action of rainwater on

Return to the village and walk up Waggon Road.

The work of a frustrated 'shooter'. The hunt (*la chasse*) is still very popular in France, so much so that there is precious little wildlife left alive!

Hector Hugh Munro

H H Munro was born on 18 December 1870 in Akyab, Burma. He was educated at Exmouth and at Bedford Grammar School. At various stages in his life he was a colonial policeman, a political satirist, a journalist, a historian, an author of novels, short stories and plays and a soldier. He is however best remembered for his fiction, for which he adopted the pen name 'Saki'. He selected this name from the Rubaiyat of Omar Khayyam, in which several sections were addressed to a 'Saki', which is the Farsi translation for cup bearer.

Munro enjoyed his childhood and even managed to raise a tiger cub, until his father, a Scottish Military Policeman, sent Hector, his sister Ethel and brother Charlie back to Scotland to be raised by two aunts. Hector was very unhappy here and regarded his aunts as tyrants. Although these aunts were probably well intentioned they brought the children up in a regime of strictness and severity. This left an indelible mark on his character and is immortalised in a number of his short stories.

Two pictures of H H Munro. He was a journalist and author and friend of Siegfried Sassoon.

He returned to Asia in his early twenties as an officer in the Colonial Burmese Military Police. He suffered with bad health, however, and had to return to England after only one year. Back in England he began to write for a variety of publications including the *Westminster Gazette*, *Daily Express*, *Bystander*, *Morning Post* and *Outlook*. Of these writings, the most notable were his parodies called 'Alice in Westminster' which were a series of political sketches for the *Westminster Gazette*. He later became a foreign correspondent in Russia and the Balkans, which is where he wrote many of the humorous short stories for which he is best remembered. He returned to London in 1908. Munro was a friend and confidante of Siegfried Sassoon and it is now widely accepted that he was homosexual.

He enlisted in the 22nd Royal Fusiliers at the start of the Great War at the age of forty-four. He refused several offers of a commission, claiming that he could not expect soldiers to follow him unless he had experience of battle. He wrote throughout his time in the trenches and was promoted to Lance Sergeant in September 1916. He was killed on 16 November 1916.

On the site of Munich Trench near the cemetery. *Feste Soden* **was in the field to the right. Ten Tree Alley ran across the middle distance. Trench lines in the fields still 'guard' the village of Serre.**

the chalk substrata. They were first utilised as a refuge during the sixteenth century wars of religion. The Germans, with typical teutonic ingenuity, developed them into extensive and relatively comfortable facilities of every description that an army required. None of the entrances here have survived, neither have those that existed in the high banking on the right as we proceed up the road, although there are several obvious points where, if it were possible to excavate, it would

Waggon Road Cemetery.

Frankfurt Trench Cemetery.

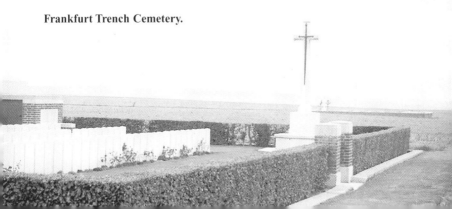

come as no surprise to find something of interest. I know of no one who knows or who is willing to admit to knowing anything about existing entrances. I am sure, however, that very substantial remains still exist.

A few years ago I was taken to another village further north from here towards Arras, and into similar excavations. Again, their origin was natural but they had been adapted by the Germans. They were very complex and ran in all directions for many kilometres. It was not a comfortable experience, though, and I was pleased to get back up the fixed ladder, which extended for about forty feet, and back into the fresh air. There was nothing of great interest left down there that I saw, although there was an area which had been used for constructing artillery shells. There was a large number of steel shell cases and a corresponding amount of explosive to pack into them, empty boxes and tins and lots of other debris. There were no fuses or nose cones; these, with their valuable metal content, had long since been removed.

Continuing up Wagon Road a turning to the left will be reached and about fifty metres beyond this was the divisional boundary with the 2nd Division. The battalions that followed the initial assault on 13 November were the 2/Oxfordshire and Buckinghamshire Light Infantry and the 17/Royal Fusiliers and it was to Wagon road that they fell back. Subsequently, all the other battalions involved in the attack over the succeeding days did likewise. This road became the new British front line, where the men formed up to make fresh attacks, although, Beaumont Trench remained as the main British position. It is, therefore, conveniently easy to be able to walk up the road, and be near the right spot as described in the battle narrative. However it is difficult to be precise because of the lack of anything tangible, even a bush, on which to give a bearing. The British position (Beaumont Trench) was an average of 300 yards to the left while the German Munich trench was about 500 yards to the right, with Frankfurt Trench beyond that, an average of about 200 yards away. New Munich Trench was the nearest in the field on the right and, as the walk progresses, came nearer to the road until after about another 500 yards from the divisional boundary point it crossed the road and continued on the other side in a half left direction.

As you emerge from the embankment, walking up the hill the small battlefield cemeteries will come into view. They seem very poignant and lonely places, the only reference points in the expansive agricultural landscape. They were built after the Germans withdrew from the area to the Hindenburg Line in 1917. Until that time the dead

The site of Munich Trench looking back over the site of the *Feste Soden* to the line of trees in Ten Tree Alley. Cemetery on the right; Pendant Copse on the left.

Pendant Copse

Ten Tree Alley Cemetery

lay out, exposed to the elements and slowly disappeared. It is hard to realise that of all the numerous battalions who were engaged in this area, of all the men who lost their lives, all that were found, when the battle field was cleared, were these men who are interred in the four cemeteries that can be seen. It is probable that more were found later over the succeeding months and years and now lie in Serre Road Number 2, the large concentration cemetery. No doubt the remains of many still lie below, but out of reach of even today's heavy farm machinery. Nearly all the major discoveries of the remains of soldiers made now are when building work of some description takes place and the earth is disturbed a few feet down. The first of these little cemeteries reached is Waggon Road Cemetery, just to the right of the road. There are 195 graves here of which forty-nine belong to 11/Border Regiment who, it will be recalled attacked here on 18 November. There are also graves of men from the 16/Lancashire Fusiliers, who attempted to rescue their colleagues of the 16/Highland Light Infantry and 11/Border Regiment who were cut off in Frankfurt Trench. Lieutenant G N Higginson was involved in that unsuccessful raid and he is buried here.

Walking further on, the access track to Munich Trench cemetery will be seen on the left. At this point you are actually standing on the site of the trench which, at this point, joined the track from right rear and continued straight ahead along the track downhill. After rain, which washes down the left of the track, it is possible to pick out trench debris, including, not surprisingly, German SAA cartridge cases. In the area to the right of the track was situated the strongpoint or redoubt, known as *Feste Soden*. Munich Trench Cemetery has 126 graves and from this position it is possible to see to the village of Serre and across to Pendant Copse. It will be recalled that it was in this area that much confusion occurred throughout the battle, when many men lost direction and found themselves mixed up with the neighbouring divisional troops. This area is also associated with Wilfred Owen who was with the 2nd Manchesters here again in January 1917. While sheltering from the bombardment in what was left of an old dugout, the man on watch at the top was hit and blinded. This was the inspiration for his well known poem, 'The Sentry'. Among those buried in Munich Trench Cemetery is Captain Heinrich William Max Thomas, a company commander with the 1/East Lancs on 1 July. Of German extraction, he must have had mixed feelings about his task that day.

There is now an option to carry on and visit Ten Tree Alley Cemetery, for which is included a separate short walk later, or retrace your steps and return to the site of the stand at Frankfurt Trench. To do the latter take the track nearly opposite the path that leads to Munich Trench Cemetery, and continue to a junction and turn right. Follow this track and take the first turn to the left. Where the track turns at the next right, stop and look ahead into the field for about twenty-five yards. The site of the famous last stand of 16/Highland Light Infantry and the 11/Borders is very close by, although there is nothing to identify the spot.

This desolate and lonely place, where possibly there are just a few relatively worthless sugar beet growing now, hardly seems a place worthy of giving up your life for. It recalls to mind my first visit to Beaumont Hamel after reading and hearing from survivors so much about that awe inspiring place that so many suffered and died for. My initial reaction was 'Is this it?'. It felt the same looking at this bit of field too. If ever there is a single place that personifies the futility of the First World War, then this must rank as one of the favourites. While at this place, note the distance to Frankfurt Trench Cemetery, which is closer to the line of Munich Trench, and this is the distance that the brave defenders of this portion of Frankfurt Trench crawled in an attempt to get some water; and not far from where Sergeant Johnstone and Private Dixon crossed Munich Trench on their successful journey back to the British lines. Of course, any prospective rescuers would have to have come from that distance, capturing and holding a part of

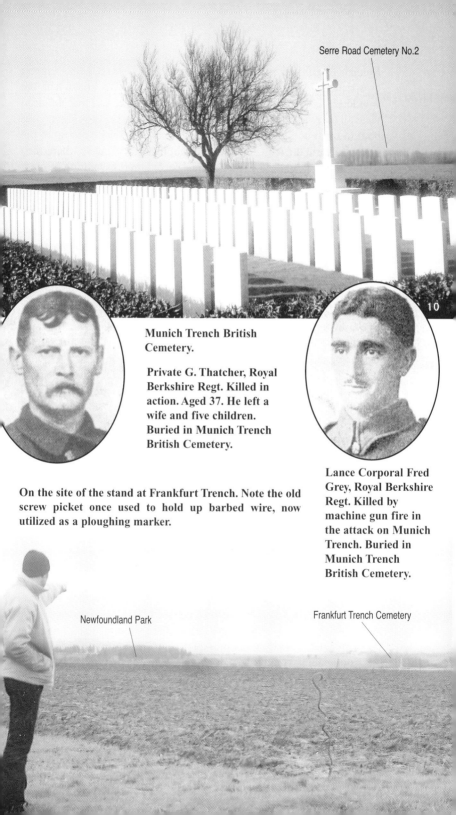

Serre Road Cemetery No.2

10

Munich Trench British Cemetery.

Private G. Thatcher, Royal Berkshire Regt. Killed in action. Aged 37. He left a wife and five children. Buried in Munich Trench British Cemetery.

On the site of the stand at Frankfurt Trench. Note the old screw picket once used to hold up barbed wire, now utilized as a ploughing marker.

Lance Corporal Fred Grey, Royal Berkshire Regt. Killed by machine gun fire in the attack on Munich Trench. Buried in Munich Trench British Cemetery.

Newfoundland Park

Frankfurt Trench Cemetery

Munich Trench which, as we know, was a task beyond them. It is sad to speculate what lies below the surface here. We know that the wounded were taken back when the stand was over and that the dead were all together in the large dugout with them. In the ensuing months both Munich and Frankfurt trenches were all but swallowed up in the mud and were difficult to locate. In all probability that is where they were left and it became a large sepulchre, but there is nothing to mark the place.

Continue back on the track, and on your left the site of Munich Trench gradually comes closer to the track as you progress, finally crossing the track and continuing on the right. Follow the track towards Frankfurt Trench Cemetery which will be seen ahead to the right. There is not always a path to the cemetery, as it sometimes gets ploughed up, but if there are crops growing and a short cut is not possible, look for the access made by the Commonwealth War Graves gardeners and follow that. The cemetery is not on or very near the site of the trench. It is, in fact, close to the site of Munich Trench, which was on the left in the field about 100 yards distant. Frankfurt Trench was about another 200 yards beyond that.

Frankfurt Trench Cemetery has a total of 134 graves, the majority belonging to the Highland Light Infantry. Among the other graves is Private J C Boon, killed in action on 16 November, a relative of the well known author Henry Williamson, who fought in the Great War. Boon was the 'model' for a character in one of Williamson's book, *The Golden Virgin,* named Percy Pickering. In the book Pickering was killed on 15 September 1916.

The last cemetery is New Munich Trench British Cemetery. This stands almost exactly on the site of the trench which was first dug by the British from this area and subsequently extended northwards, on the right of Wagon Road, and became the jumping off position for the later assaults. There are 146 graves, the majority belonging to the 16/Highland Light Infantry and the 17/Highland Light Infantry and it was in this area that both those battalions were badly caught by their own barrage on 18 November. To be fair to the gunners, their batteries near Mailly Maillet were situated behind a sloping ridge and were firing on to a reverse slope in some cases. Visibility was almost non existent and observation not possible.

At this point Munich Trench was closest to New Munich Trench, at some places only about 150 yards, but the British troops were still unable to get in.

A contemporary report written by an angry officer of the

17/Highland Light Infantry stated:

> *What is clear, is that the British barrage was hopelessly off target. As if the extreme cold and snow, and later the sleet was not enough, the initial barrage which was intended to fall in front of the troops lying out in No Man's Land, waiting to attack, actually fell right on top of them. Even when it was supposed to lift for the final four minutes directly on to Munich Trench, it was still 50 yards short with the result that those attackers who survived the initial blunder were still under fire from their own guns while the Germans manning Munich Trench in large numbers were not inconvenienced and opened fire with their machine guns. With this handicap the assault was doomed to failure before it had begun.*

Ten Tree Alley

The Royal Garrison Artillery in action at Mailly-Maillet.

An extra visit can be made, if desired, to this rather remote little place, but it is worth the effort. It can be reached easily enough on foot while visiting Munich Trench Cemetery, or it is possible to get nearer by car, by using the road between Beaucourt sur l'Ancre and Serre, from where there is a track that may be passable by car, but a walk would ensure a problem free visit. Interestingly, when I last visited, there were ten mature trees growing nearby, but with the French penchant for cutting down any thing that could possibly, however minutely, augment the supply of firewood, it cannot be guaranteed that they will still be there. It is, though, a rewarding visit, and a beautiful little place in a shallow valley, so different from the other cemeteries described.

The cemetery is situated on the bank above the site of the long German communication trench from which it is named. There are sixty-seven graves and the 11/Borders, from the attack of 18 November, are well represented. Other graves date from the attacks made in February 1917 by other battalions of the same division and the 62nd (West Riding) Division. By that time, both Munich and Frankfurt trenches had ceased to exist and were mere depressions in the ground over which the attacking troops passed without realising they had done so. The only indication of the sites was a series of unconnected posts, some of which were unmanned at night, that the Germans maintained, probably the site of their best dugouts that had not been overwhelmed by the mud. An interesting anecdote is worth recalling here of an incident that occurred on Christmas Day 1916.

On 17 December, 22 Brigade (7th Division) had the misfortune to be sent into the front line with the prospect of occupation throughout the Christmas period. All four battalions covered the whole divisional sector from Ten Tree Alley in the north to the Beaumont-Beaucourt road in the south. Among these was the 1/Royal Welsh Fusiliers. A Captain Blennerhasset had an idea that he thought might foreshorten the war and enable everyone to go 'home' for Christmas, well, at least, start packing up. On Christmas Day he persuaded a fellow officer, Second Lieutenant Freeman, to go across No Man's Land to the German trenches and get them to surrender. There had been no firing and they set off carrying a suitable piece of white material, a 'white flag', and arrived safely and unharmed at their destination. The report merely states that he made this journey and returned 'without success'. It would have been fascinating to know more. How long did they stay, what was said and what language was spoken. Perhaps, from his name, we might deduce that our gallant captain was of German extraction.

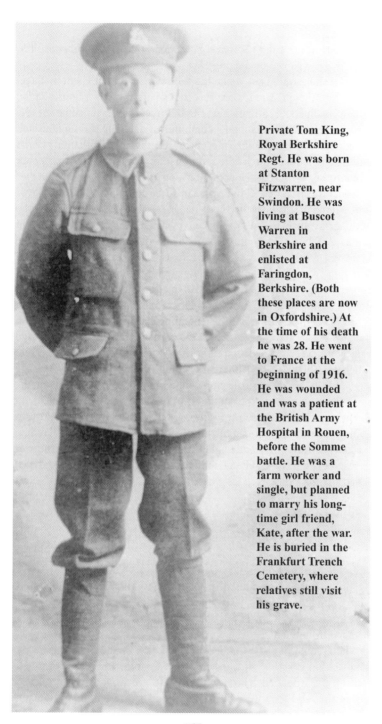

Private Tom King, Royal Berkshire Regt. He was born at Stanton Fitzwarren, near Swindon. He was living at Buscot Warren in Berkshire and enlisted at Faringdon, Berkshire. (Both these places are now in Oxfordshire.) At the time of his death he was 28. He went to France at the beginning of 1916. He was wounded and was a patient at the British Army Hospital in Rouen, before the Somme battle. He was a farm worker and single, but planned to marry his long-time girl friend, Kate, after the war. He is buried in the Frankfurt Trench Cemetery, where relatives still visit his grave.

Let's hope at least the Germans gave them a drink of schnapps! The brigade was relieved on Boxing Day.

It is a short walk back down the hill into Beaumont Hamel village. Just before the cross roads are reached, where there is a house on the corner, is the site of another filled up entrance to some of the underground tunnels that honeycomb the village. The private house on the corner was once a thriving café, catering for the visitors to the battlefields, a trade which faded away as the years passed, but now well evidenced again across the area.

General Sir Hubert Gough continued to command the Fifth Army until March 1918 when he took the blame for the retreat before the German advance. He was replaced by General Rawlinson and sent home. After the war, he remained in obscurity. I met, on the battlefields, just a few years ago, Edwin Clabburn, whose father had served in World War One and following in his father's footsteps joined the yeomanry in the late twenties. He lived in Chelsea quite near to Sir Hubert Gough and used to see him about, often carrying a brown paper carrier bag in which he had his shopping. He frequented a local pub and always sat on the same stool in the corner, but if anyone recognised him they never acknowledged him. My friend never approached him either. He seemed a lonely figure. Gough's only other local activity seemed to be to get his golf clubs out and practice a few shots on the grass in the gardens in the square where he lived.

He must have had some friends, though. In the middle thirties a 'lobby' grew up and campaigned for Gough's 'reinstatement', claiming he had been unfairly treated. This succeeded when, in 1937 he was awarded the G.C.M.G. Gough outlived all his contemporaries and died as recently as 1963, aged 92.

OTHER PLACES TO VISIT

Sucrerie Military Cemetery

As the battalions featured in this book were relieved so they took their wounded with them. Those that were too ill to move any further were left behind, so it is possible to find casualties of battles some distance from the place where the action took place. The nearest place to where some of the wounded were taken was the Sucrerie, on the road to Mailly Maillet. It was here that the motor ambulances came to pick up the wounded. Those with very severe wounds never made it any further and they were buried in the cemetery that takes its name from the then ruined sugar refinery. Today it is a prosperous farm and holiday 'hostel' for young people. The cemetery had been prepared for its anticpated occupants, and graves were already dug as the men marched past up the lane from Colincamps to the front line.

Here will be found many headstones of men who belong to the battalions mentioned in this book, including two commanding officers of the 4th Division, Lieutenant Colonel J A Thickness of the 1/Somerset Light Infantry and Lieutenant Colonel L W Palk DSO of the 1/Hampshires.

Mailly Maillet Communal Extension

It was in the fields around this cemetery that the unfortunate members of the battalions attacking in November found themselves

Sucrerie Military Cemetery.

Captain B S Smith-Masters MC, Essex Regiment, is buried in the Sucrerie Military Cemetery.

Second Lieutenant M H Blackwood, Seaforth Highlanders, is buried in the Sucrerie Military Cemetery.

Second Lieutenant N T Ide, Essex Regiment, is buried in the Sucrerie Military Cemetery.

Captain G N Alison, Seaforth Highlanders, is buried in the Sucrerie Military Cemetery.

Captain H W Sayres, 2/ Lancashire Fusiliers, is buried in the Sucrerie Military Cemetery.

Captain C C Ford, adjutant of the 1/Somerset Light Infantry, killed 1 July with his commanding officer, Lieutenant Colonel J Thicknesse (right), and buried near him in the Sucrerie Military Cemetery.

bivouacked without any food. The cemetery is quite small and was not used extensively, having only 116 graves.

Mailly Wood Cemetery

The first 1916 burials here were a group of men of the 2/Seaforth Highlanders, who were killed by a German shell of a counter bombardment during the British preliminary artillery action to the battle of the Somme, on 25 June 1916. There are many subsequent burials from the July-November period. Care should be exercised if attempting to drive down the track to the site as it is very bumpy and there is limited turning space.

Louvencourt Military Cemetery

This cemetery is a little further afield, out on the road to Doullens, but is well worth a visit. It is the burial place of Brigadier General C B Prowse DSO, commanding 11 Brigade who was anxious to get into a forward position and as we have seen went forward too soon and was severely wounded. According to the brigade report he was taken to Marieux. As he lay dying he made the well reported comment: 'I did not before think much of territorials, but by God, they can fight.' In Belgium, near 'Plugstreet' Wood, there is a cemetery known as Prowse Point, named after the general. There was also a farm named after him at the time of his exploits in October 1914, as battalion commander of the 1/Somersets, for which he was promoted to Lieutenant Colonel and awarded the DSO.

Also buried here is Second Lieutenant Roland Leighton, who was the fiancée of Vera Brittain. Their story is very well known, and Vera Brittain, the mother of politican, Dame Shirley Williams, wrote extensively of her experiences, especially in *Testament of Youth* in which

Brigadier General C B Prowse DSO.

171

**Second Lieutenant
Roland Leighton.**

she describes visiting the cemetery.

Private H MacDonald of the West Yorkshire Regiment had served with distinction in the South African campaign. When his wife in Keighley fell seriously ill, he applied unsuccessfully for compassionate leave. He absconded several times to get back to Yorkshire to see his wife. He was subsequently court martialled and shot at dawn.

Vera Brittain.

SELECTIVE INDEX

Capt G N Alison	170
Lt R F Andrews	66
George Ashurst	145, 154
Capt C E Baird	134
Major G W Barclay MC	29
Black Prince The	109 - 117
2 Lt M H Blackwood	170
Pte J C Boon	166
Lt V A Braithwaite	132
Vera Brittain	171
Major J Bromilow	32, 35
Lt F C Caird	92
Capt C G Carson	52
Sgt A H Cook	27, 28, 39 - 41, 128
Lt Col F P Crozier	143
Pte J Crozier	143, 144
Lt W Daly	23, 24
Pte J T Dixon	86, 87, 162
W F E East	66
Edward III	109 - 117
2 Lt H L Field	134
Lt Col G Fitzgerald	43, 44
Marshal F Foch	9, 10
Capt C C Ford	170
Lt G W Glover DSO	29, 30, 38, 39, 128
Lt F Goldsmith	47
Sir Hubert Gough	47, 65, 66, 69, 71, 91, 108, 109
Norman Gray	96
Lt Col J S Green DSO	19
Lance Cpl F Grey	163
Sgt A Hackett	79
Sir Douglas Haigh	7, 8, 9, 12, 47, 60, 65, 66, 143
Lt A A S Hamilton	57
Sgt H Hargreaves	18
Lt V S F Hawkins	32, 35, 36, 44
Capt S H Heath	24
Lt G N Higginson	92, 162
Lt Col J O Hopkinson	36, 39
2 Lt N T Ide	170
C S M S M Johnstone	86, 87, 162
Marshal J C C Joffre	7 - 9
Pte T King	167
Sgt G A Lee	96
Capt S W Ludlow	134, 136
Col W R Ludlow	134 - 140
Pte H MacDonald	172
Capt B C Smith Masters	170
Capt C W Merryweather	91, 92
A A Milne	60
Lance Sgt H Munro	157, 158
Lt R Newcombe	22
Wilfred Owen	162
2 Lt W J Page	22 - 24
Lt Col the Hon L W Palk DSO	25, 171
Cpl T R Parker	47
Pte T H Philpot	58
Sgt J E Preston	96
Pte J Priestley	120
Brig Gen C B Prowse	34, 35, 171
Drummer W Richie VC	39, 128, 157
Lt H B Rylands	92
Capt H W Sayres	170
Lt E D Shearn	25, 26,

42, 43
Lt Col Sir George Stirling   33, 35
2 Lt G C Stoneham   56

Pte G Thatcher   163
Lt Col J A Thicknesse   27, 170
Capt H W M Thomas   162
Major Townsend   30, 31

Lance Cpl J Veitch   94

Capt A Weatherhead   33
Dame Shirley Williams   172
Henry Williamson   166

PLACE NAMES
Albert   105, 118
8/Argyll & Sutherland Memorial
    144
Beaumont-Hamel 45, 52, 55, 69,
    119, 141, 144, 156, 168
Beaumont Trench 18, 27, 29, 33,
    34, 50, 51-55, 152, 160
Bradford Pals 129, 131
Chambres d' Hôtes   107
Crécy   109-118
Feste Soden   31, 36,
    74, 75, 80, 159-162
Frankfurt Trench   36, 47,
    52, 53, 59, 69-71, 80-100,
    161-166
Frankfurt Trench Cemetery 159
Frontier Lane   127
Gloucester Cathedral   116, 117
Hawthorn Ridge/Crater 12-14, 18,
    48, 144, 154
Hotels   107
Leeds Pals   16, 131
Louvencourt Military Cemetery
    171
Mailly-Maillet   63, 64,
    67, 71, 91, 143
Mailly-Maillet Comm Ext
Cemetery 171
Mailly Wood Cemetery   171
Munich Trench   18, 27,
    29 - 34, 47, 52, 55 - 59, 67, 69,
    70, 74 - 80, 161 - 167
Munich Trench Cemetery 159
New Munich Trench   70, 161
New Munich Trench Cemetery
    165 - 167
Pendant Copse   18, 32,
    36, 76
Quadrilateral   16, 27, 33,
    38 - 42, 51 - 55, 64, 65, 127
    - 133, 159
Redan Ridge Cemetery No 1
    124 - 126
Redan Ridge Cemetery No 2
    120, 121
Redan Ridge Cemetery No 3
    122 - 124, 127
Ridge Redoubt 15, 16, 18, 26, 27,
    33, 36, 38, 122, 124
Serre   18, 31,
    35, 52 - 55, 64 - 65, 127 - 133,
    159
Serre Road Cemetery No 1   126 -
    128, 139
Serre Road Cemetery No 2   126,
    127, 132 - 140
Sucrerie Military Cemetery   164,
    168, 169
Sunken Road   142 - 147

Ten Tree Alley   34, 36,
    53, 128, 159, 161, 162, 167, 168
Wagon Road   34, 52,
    59, 60, 70, 157, 159, 160, 162
Waggon Road Cemetery   159
Watling Street   22, 25, 32,
    36, 42, 43, 120, 138, 141
White City   63, 64,
    87, 145, 148

BATTALIONS
6/Bedfordshire   59
1/Royal Berkshire   54, 57
11/Border   73, 78 -
    80, 83 - 100, 162, 168
2/Royal Dublin Fusiliers   11, 18,
    32, 33, 38, 148

2/Duke of Wellingtons 11, 18, 32 - 34, 141
1/East Lancashire 11, 16, 18, 19, 24, 32, 142, 147
8/East Lancashire 66 - 68
2/Essex 11, 16, 18, 32 - 34, 129, 141
13/Essex 48, 52, 121
17/Royal Fusiliers 48, 50, 56, 160
22/Royal Fusiliers 53, 55, 59, 64, 65, 158, 159
24/Royal Fusiliers 48 - 50, 156
1/Hampshire 11, 18, 24 - 26, 132, 141, 147
2/Highland Light Infantry 48 - 50, 64, 156
15/Highland Light Infantry 73, 75
16/Highland Light Infantry 73, 78, 81, 83 - 100, 162, 167
17/Highland Light Infantry 72, 73 - 77, 167
1/Royal Irish Fusiliers 11, 18, 36, 43
2/Inniskillings 91
1/Kings Liverpool 48, 52,
1/Kings Own 11, 16, 18, 32 - 35, 129, 140
2/Kings Own Yorkshire L I 73 -78, 83
1/Kings Royal Rifle Corps 54 - 57, 59, 64
1/Lancashire Fusiliers 145, 149 - 151
2/Lancashire Fusiliers 1, 16, 18, 32 - 36
16/Lancashire Fusiliers 91, 162
10/Loyal North Lancashire 67, 68
2/Manchester 73, 74, 162

17/Middlesex 48, 51-53
2/Oxford & Buckinghamshire LI 46, 50, 52, 55, 160
1/Rifle Brigade 11, 18, 26, 29, 38, 129, 140
2/Seaforth Highlanders 11, 18, 33, 36, 40, 141, 148
1/Somerset L I 11, 18, 27, 33, 140, 141
2/South Staffordshire 48, 51-54
1/Royal Warwickshire 11, 18, 38, 141
6/Royal Warwickshire 16, 18, 30, 32, 129, 140
8/Royal Warwickshire 16, 18, 30 - 32, 39, 129
11/Royal Warwickshire 59

BRIGADES
5 Brigade 48 - 49
6 Brigade 48 - 59
10 Brigade 11 - 44
11 Brigade 11 - 44
12 Brigade 11 - 44
14 Brigade 74
96 Brigade 91
97 Brigade 73

DIVISIONS
2 Division 46 - 59, 70, 103
3 Division 51, 53, 70
4 Division 11 - 44
18 Division 45
29 Division 12 - 15
31 Division 16, 36
32 Division 68 - 71, 80
37 Division 59, 67
39 Division 45
49 Division 45
51 Division 48, 51, 56 69, 70, 119

ACKNOWLEDGEMENTS

I would like to acknowledge the support and co-operation of the following individuals and organisations/institutions in the preparation of this book

Nick Arber; Stephanie Bennett, Royal Warwickshire Regimental Museum; Reverend Nigel Cave; Dr Roger Custance, Winchester College; Lt Colonel C D Darroch, Royal Hampshire Regimental Museum; Peter Donnelly, King's Own Regimental Museum; Lt Colonel John Downham, Queen's Lancashire Regiment; Lt Colonel David Eliot, Somerset Light Infantry Regimental Museum; Norman Gray; Frederick Hackett; Gordon Hawkesworth;
John & Sheila Iles; Amanda Mareno, Royal Irish Regimental Fusiliers Museum; Emma Renshaw; Helen Renshaw; Julie Renshaw; Dr John Robb; Colonel Jack Sheldon, Queen's Lancashire Regiment; Karl Simpson; Gary Smith, Museum of the Queen's Lancashire Regiment, Michael & Frances Speakman; Liz Tait; Kyle Tallett; James W Taylor; Robert Thompson; Roni Wilkinson, Pen & Sword Books; Yousef Al-Shawa; The British Newspaper Library; The Imperial War Museum; The National Archives.